S0-CWV-178

THE
CAREGIVER
MEDITATIONS

THE
CAREGIVER
MEDITATIONS

Reflections on Loving Presence

ERIE CHAPMAN

Copyright © 2008 by Erie Chapman

All rights reserved. No part of this book may be used or reproduced in any manner whatsoever without written permission except in the case of brief quotations embodied in critical articles and reviews.

Printed in the United States of America

Library of Congress Control Number: Pending

ISBN 978-0-9800664-0-1

Third Printing - 2008

Cover Painting: Highmore, Joseph *The Good Samaritan,* 1744. Tate Gallery, London, Great Britain. Photo credit: Tate Gallery, London.

Printed at Vaughn Printing, Nashville

Published by:
      Baptist Healing Trust and
      October Hill Press, an imprint of
      The Erie Chapman Foundation

Distributed by:
      Baptist Healing Trust
      1919 Charlotte Avenue, Suite 320
      Nashville, Tennessee 37204
      615.284.8271
      www.healinghospital.org
      www.eriechapman.com

OTHER WORKS BY ERIE CHAPMAN

Books:
Life is Choices, Choose Well (CHI Press, 1995)
Radical Loving Care: Building the Healing Hospital in America (BHT, 2003, also an Audio Book, 2006)
Scotty the Snail – A Children's Book (Grandparents Press, 2004)
Sacred Work: Planting Radical Loving Care in America (BHT, 2006)

Films:
Acts of Caring – Produced and Directed by Erie Chapman (1993)
Sacred Work – (Baptist Healing Trust, 2001) – Produced and Directed by Erie Chapman; Editor, Van Grafton; Videography, Van Grafton and Andrew Haege
The Servant's Heart – the lives of four caregivers (Baptist Healing Trust, 2003) – Produced and Directed by Erie Chapman; Editor, Van Grafton; Director of Videography, Van Grafton

Music compositions:
Blessed Baby. . . and Other Sacred Music of Healing (Baptist Healing Trust, 2003)
Angel Hour (2003)
The Quiet Piano (2004)

All of the above are available through:
www.healinghospital.com

Or through:
The Baptist Healing Trust
Nashville, Tennessee

Dedication

This work is dedicated to America's caregivers, especially

Tracy, Cathy, Deadre, Laura, Keith, Roy, Liz, Cheryl,

Lorraine, Marian, Karen, Mary Lynne and all those

who have devoted their life work to the care of others.

Always act out of love, not fear.

SYMBOL OF LOVING SERVICE

Loving care has a long and beautiful tradition in human history. In these pages the heritage of loving care is symbolized by the image of a Golden Thread, which is also a symbol of faith in God. It represents the positive tradition of healing versus the negative tradition of transaction-based behavior.

A pair of intersecting circles signifies the merging of love and need in the Sacred Encounter, which is the fundamental relationship between caregiver and patient. This symbol also signifies hope—the hope that comes into our hearts when we experience loving encounters.

A red heart signifies the nature of the Servant's Heart. It also symbolizes love and is love's greatest expression. This expression, although it specifically references the heart, assumes the full involvement of our best thought processes. Loving care is not loving if it fails to engage the best skills and competency of caregivers.

CONTENTS

INTRODUCTION

REFLECTIONS ON LOVING

THE PRESENCE MEDITATIONS

About Presence

The Arts Teach Presence

Nature Teaches Presence

INTRODUCTION

THE POWER OF THE MEDITATION HABIT— ENRICHING YOUR LIFE WITH NEWS FROM YOUR HEART

It is only with the heart that one can see rightly; what is essential is invisible to the eye.

—from *The Little Prince* by Antoine de St. Exupery

In Antoine de St. Exupery's charming and now eternal story, a little prince goes searching strange lands. Toward the end of the story, he is advised by a wise fox that one can only see the truth with the heart.

In today's healthcare world, governed so powerfully by measurement-oriented science, how can we learn to attend to our belief in that which is "invisible to the eye"? How can we listen more closely to the news from our hearts?

One way for us to do this is to begin asking questions that plumb the depths of our priorities. What are the days that stand out most in your life? What are the moments that are etched so vividly in your memory that you find yourself calling them up in exact detail as if they happened yesterday?

For some, there are the obvious things—births, deaths, weddings, national disasters like 911, or, if you're old enough, the Kennedy or King assassinations.

What of the other days? What about the thousands of days you have lived for which you have no real recollection? Do you remember your 23rd birthday or the day after it? Do you remember how you passed the twenty-four hours you lived, say, two months ago or two weeks ago?

If we're healthy and have held the same job for a long time, our days may become matter-of-fact experiences—parts of them lived so automatically and unthinkingly that they become like the drive to work. We see but don't notice. We hear but don't listen.

That's not how days feel to patients with life-threatening illnesses who live now in hospices, hospitals, and nursing homes. One of the first things the dying emphasize is the precious quality of each day—how they notice the minutes. How they rise and watch the dawn, how they dwell in the aroma of roses sent by friends. For these beings, the news from the heart is all that matters.

What the devil is wrong with the rest of us? Does it require the imminent threat of our own death for us to finally become present to our own lives?

I want to urge you to acquire the meditation habit, because we all need reminders from our hearts. One way is to read a meditation every day, perhaps from a book of meditations like this one. Some may wish to read the online version of this collection, the *Journal of Sacred Work*. Many people have found that logging on to the *Journal* is a wonderful way to begin their

day; others find that it provides a few welcome moments of rest at the end of the day. Read and meditate as a way of reawakening *your own wisdom*. So many of us live away from the truth of our hearts, fearful of being hurt, or unsure of the power that lies within each of us.

The five or ten minutes you may spend each day reading and meditating and, hopefully, *keeping your own journal*, offer a marvelous way to learn presence to the day and to your life. Find more time for this, for if you do, your life will be enriched. This kind of journaling is not just about recording the news of what you *did* that day—your trip to the store, what you had for dinner, the temperature. It's about *the news of your heart* and what you are learning about your loves, your joys, your sorrows. In other words, the crucial yet invisible truths of your life.

The Bible records turning-point moments in the lives of saints, prophets, and other luminous figures. Paul's illumination on his trip to Damascus; Moses' trip down from Mt. Sinai with the Ten Commandments; the miracle of Christ's birth, death, and resurrection. Other books of faith record turning-point moments in the history of the spirit.

What about those of us who are ordinary people? What are the epiphanies that mark our lives and call us to remember that we lived a certain day in a certain way? Epiphanies come to those whose hearts are open to them.

The art of living is exactly that—an art. It requires attention, education, and most of all, exquisite presence. Don't let the news on television interfere with your attention to the news of your own life. We each have the

chance to remember this very day by how we live it and what we choose to remember in our writing. The way we live this day can enrich the lives of others and ourselves and provide nourishment for our days and nights.

What is the most important thing you will do on this day (or have done already?) How will it enrich the life of another? The choice is in your hands—each moment of your days. What is the news from your heart right now? Write this news in your journal so you may watch, reflect, and grow as a caregiver and as a person.

To help with the daily journal habit, visit the online Journal of Sacred Work, *where you will find daily caregiver meditations and reports of best practices in hospitals and charities. Enter* www.journalofsacredwork.typepad.com *in your browser and bookmark the site or add it to your Favorites.*

PRINCIPLES OF LOVING CARE—THE PERSON IN THE MIRROR

Love, allowing the other to be a legitimate other, is the only emotion that expands intelligence.

—Dr. Humberto Maturana, neurobiologist and co-inventor of autopoiesis

Leafing through the scrapbook of early life moments, we may come across images of early incarnations of ourselves. Who is that little fellow in the black-and-white photograph? I asked myself that when I came across this image from 1949. I know it's me, digging along the Pacific shoreline, my mother and two sisters nearby. But that me is also gone. Where did he go?

Our physical "child" has vanished along with the young body that housed our spirits back then. And yet that child lives still, hiding somewhere behind our aging faces along with all the other people we have been in our lives. It is as children that we first learned about love. As adults we seek to understand this power we have and how to express it.

Maturana has written that *living is a process of cognition*. We act on what we have learned and how we perceive reality. From the time we are infants, our cognition, or awareness, is constantly changing. We study the world around us for clues about who we are and often wonder at the answers. Who is the person we see in the mirror today? Is it a being in Love or a being in fear? It is, of course, both. Living Love means shifting the balance within us so that we become more present to the power of love and more distant from the threats of fear.

I usually don't like lists because they seem to convert mysterious and hallowed principles into overly simple phrases. I'm also not sure that lists of things really change behavior. But what they can accomplish is *awakening* those who are truly interested in participating in genuine change. So I have created a list of seven personal Loving Care concepts, each just a few words long, in the hope that they will be starting points for reflection and guiding principles along our journey to loving presence.

Love's First Principle: **Live Love, Not Fear.** This is your life's purpose. Love is the divine spark planted in us by God. Let that spark shine in your life, extinguishing the darkness of fear.

Love's Second Principle: **Where Attention Goes, Energy Flows.** By attending to your energy, you can change your life.

Love's Third Principle: **Take Care of Yourself So You Can Take Care of Others.** Self-care is essential to other-care.

Love's Fourth Principle: **Live Your Calling by Being Present to Life.** As Kierkegaard said, we are all born with sealed orders. Open yours.

Love's Fifth Principle: **Follow Guiding Principles, Not Rules.** The world is too complex to live by rules. Rules call us to be robots. Guiding principles appeal to our humanity and our ability to think, reflect, and allow God to work in our lives.

Love's Sixth Principle: **Take Your Work Seriously, Not Yourself.** Humor and humility about ourselves allows us to stay balanced. Without these, we may confuse the living of godly work with being a god.

Love's Seventh Principle: **Live in Gratitude.** Follow this principle and joy will be your regular companion. Some believe that it is the most important principle.

These seven practices are intended to change cognition, to affect the way in which we interpret life and live love. And there should really be an eighth: *Practice all of these principles all of the time.*

Love's First Principle

Live Love, Not Fear

Everybody says they believe in love. But how well are we doing being present to love's light? The primary principle of loving care is contained in a single four-word phrase: *Live love, not fear.* That this is a difficult concept to practice becomes clear when we review the number of decisions we make out of fear—self-interest, fear for our lives, fear for our livelihoods.

Remarkably, we are born with only two fears: of falling and of loud noises. All other fears are learned. We learn fear of things that threaten our lives. Soon afterwards, we learn fear of punishment and fear of things that threaten our livelihood. To recover our presence to love requires conscious cognitive practices.

Why isn't the pattern of choosing love over fear already ingrained in us? Part of this has to do with how we were raised and how peer pressure continues to influence our thinking. Who were we as children? What were our dreams and insights? Who are we as adults?

C.S. Lewis wrote in *Mere Christianity:*

> Do not waste your time bothering whether you 'love' your neighbor, act as if you did. As soon as we do this, we find one of the great secrets. When you are behaving as if you loved someone, you will presently come to love him. If you injure someone you dislike, you will find yourself disliking him more. If you do him a good turn, you will find yourself disliking him less.

The only way to fail the test of sacred work and of life is not to take it—to retreat to the stands and watch passion playing out on the field before us.

What is the challenge for every caregiver in the world? It is always tempting to run away, to rest where we are, to give in to inertia and stop trying, to ignore the need of another and dwell in ourselves. The challenge is to keep trying—because the person before you needs your strength.

The gift of life is the gift of love. The only way to live love is to live with

passion, to take the field with all its suffering and joy and the demands of others who need our love. And to know, at the end, that we have made our best effort to improve the lives of others and that we, ourselves, have lived and we have loved. This is the chance life offers to us.

Love's Second Principle

Where Attention Goes, Energy Flows

Intuition is more important than IQ . . . I never discovered anything with my rational mind.

—Albert Einstein

E instein was the man with the wild hair and the brain of a genius. In one famous photograph, this genius sticks his tongue out at us. Einstein's wisdom changed the understanding of energy in the world. His insights can help us focus on the direction of our *human* energy.

We are born with a certain level of intuition. Education teaches us to use our rational capability to analyze problems. Now, along comes one of the greatest thinkers in history telling us to solve problems through *intuition* rather than through rationality—to stick our tongues out at traditional analytical problem-solving.

The great genius is appealing to us to relearn what we knew as small children. Trust the wisdom of our intuition. This doesn't mean ignoring the facts. It means putting intuition in balance with rationality.

Where attention goes, energy flows. More than a nice rhyme, this statement can change our lives. It can awaken us to the awareness of the energy flowing through us and how we might redirect it. Intuitively, we know that various kinds of powerful energy flow through us each day. We can attend to this energy or ignore it.

Imagine that you are driving to work and someone cuts you off. The energy of anger rises within you. How long will you allow that energy to dominate your life? A moment, a minute, an hour? Subconsciously, you know that you are in charge of your thoughts and you wouldn't want to yield this power to another—especially a stranger you can't even see. Consciously, you are angry.

Awareness of the principle of the value of your positive energy may enable you to shake your primitive retaliative response and convert that energy from negative to positive. A cognitive process may put you back in

touch with the wisdom of your intuition and the problem of negative energy may begin to be resolved.

Interested in opening the doors of your life to more positive energy? Let's go one step further in this journey.

Consider the flow of positive and negative energy through you each day. If you are experiencing excessive stress, it may be that you are allowing certain forces to dominate your life. You can change that. Assume there is someone in your life you think of as an enemy. Every time you think of this person, you feel the poison of hostility rising within you, drop by drop. In a way, your thoughts are arming your enemy with toxins with which he or she is hurting you. The more you think of your enemy with hostility, the more poison flows through you.

How do you change that energy? Martin Luther King Jr. said that *the only way to convert an enemy into a friend is through love*. The short

answer to cutting off the poison you are allowing your enemy to pour into you is by changing your thoughts to something more positive. But this may be a temporary solution. A deeper pathway is to *rethink your idea of this person*. He or she was once a baby who, like you, was born with the divine spark. This awareness does not require that you endorse this person's behavior, but it does call us to remember the fundamental humanity of the other. For in the course of our anger, we may have begun to objectify our enemy, converting him or her from a person to an "it," a sort of devil, a thing.

And this is what Martin Buber was talking about when he talked about the human passage from "I-it" to "I-thou," a personal transformation in which we see the other person holistically as someone with whom we relate at the most human level. This passage is central to living love. We need to move our energy to an awareness of the other from it to thou.

In our day-to-day lives, we can dissolve the toxin of hatred by redirecting our energy into far more positive pathways. By consciously opening ourselves to the light of love, we can allow love's energy to surge through us, driving away some of the darkness and dissolving hatred's poison.

This is why it is so important that we become present to this second principle. Where is your energy right now? Einstein tells us that $E = mc^2$. More important, he tells us that the real answer is not in the formula on the blackboard but in our heart's intuition.

The human energy formula is: Love = our energy × God's.

So ask yourself this question many times across the day: where is

my energy right now? As a caregiver, this single question may help you to re-energize your life by consciously invoking new patterns of positive thinking.

This doesn't mean you become Mary Poppins. It doesn't mean you ignore suffering and sadness. It means you allow energy to bring you courage, light, and compassion. It means you become a person who lives love.

Love's Third Principle

Take Care of Yourself So You Can Take Care of Others

If we lose cabin pressure, oxygen masks will drop down. If you are traveling with a small child or someone else who needs assistance, put the mask on yourself first so that you will be able to help the other person.

— FAA required announcement on all airline flights

The first time I paid attention to this announcement was more than thirty years ago. I was traveling with my then six-week-old son. The announcement startled me because I had been thinking that I would certainly put the mask on our baby first, not on myself.

Caregivers need this same reminder. In the course of our dedication, we may forget to put the mask of self-care on ourselves so that we will have the strength and energy to help others. We need oxygen before we can give it. *We need to love ourselves before we can love others.*

True serenity will never come from a place outside us. As caregivers, we need first to find this serenity *within* us so that we may bring it to both ourselves and to others.

The greatest wisdom around daily self-care is contained in one of the best and most helpful prayers ever written. Most of us know this as the Serenity Prayer, composed by the late Reinhold Niebuhr. It is an integral part of most addiction recovery programs. Yet we need to integrate its wisdom into all of our lives. Here it is again:

> *God grant me the serenity*
> *to accept the things I cannot change;*
> *courage to change the things I can;*
> *and wisdom to know the difference.*

It's a short prayer, easy to memorize, hard to live. One of the wisest and most important things you can do today is to memorize this prayer and to incorporate it into your daily meditation.

We may reflect on this prayer by considering its three elements.

1) **Serenity.** It seems obvious that we should not bother about things beyond our control. Yet how many of the things we worry about each day are in this category? The major faiths offer serenity through surrendering to God, to submitting to the grace and love this power represents. Surrender may be symbolized in physical actions. Moslems lean forward toward the east on hands and knees five times a day to symbolize submission to God. Jews and Christians bow their heads in prayer. Buddhists close their eyes. Submission is difficult because it means letting go—surrendering our will to God's—and then letting come. This requires both remembering and practicing. Most of us identify serenity more easily through an image like relaxing into a hammock on a nice summer's day.

Fortunately, we don't need a hammock to find serenity. We can find it within ourselves in the world that lives behind our closed eyes. After a time of rest and self-care, we carry the aroma of our renewed grace throughout the rest of the day, allowing its fragrance to inform some part of the world's heart.

2) **Courage.** The second part of the prayer is love's call to us to find courage. Specifically, love calls us to use this courage to change the things we can. What are these things? The first has to do with our own attitude. Love calls us to see ourselves as children of God, to see all others in the same light, and to open our hearts to serving love by serving others. What can I change with the mere power of my humanity? I can teach myself to be an instrument of love. This means allowing myself to be used by love to change the condition of another—to help another to heal. As every caregiver knows, this takes courage, the courage to surrender to love's call and the courage to act.

3) **Wisdom.** The wisdom called for in the last part of the prayer is the insight to know the difference between what I can change and what I cannot. Every day, millions of us waste energy fretting about things beyond our control. We worry about everything from the weather to the behavior of other people over whom we have no influence at all. Indeed, enormous amounts of human stress flow from the desire of many of us to try to change other people. It's difficult enough to change ourselves much less trying to re-mold the personalities of others.

In any case, *the two best ways* to bring the kind of awakening that will change others for the better have nothing to do with control. The two best ways are contained in advice I got from the late minister Waldemar Argow. When our son was young, I asked him about parenting. He said, "I can summarize all of my parenting advice in one word: example."

A few years later, I learned the second key. It's also contained in a single word: presence.

I offer these gifts to you today. Notice the *example* you are setting for others as well as yourself. And practice full *presence* to others.

These gifts are best unwrapped by integrating the Serenity Prayer into our lives. The more often we reflect on this three-part prayer, the more illumination will enter our lives. Gradually, the prayer will mirror back to us thought patterns that are wasting our energy and reflect positive patterns that are energizing. In *serenity,* we are in touch with love and think more clearly. Through this resonance between us and our mirror, the prayer helps us align with the energy of *courage*. We may enter the land of *wisdom* that shows us when to let go, allowing the best energy of ourselves to *change the things we can!*

Take care of yourself. Breathe in love's oxygen. You are a child of God.

Love's Fourth Principle

Live Your Calling by Being Present to Life

Presence to our calling is presence to Love.

—E.C.

Søren Kierkegaard (1813–1855) wrote: "The thing is to find a truth which is true for me, to find the idea for which I can live and die."

A truth for which we *can live and die*? This sounds very dramatic for those of us who may think of our lives as ordinary. But the fact is that we will live part of our lives in careers anyway, so why not discover our personal truth—the thing for which we *will* live for and ultimately die, our calling? Kierkegaard, one of the great existentialist philosophers, is reported to have suggested that we were all born with sealed orders. It's a powerful image, isn't it? How do we know what our orders are? Kierkegaard warns that we cannot simply "tear open" the special dispatch God has planted within us. We must discover our orders—find our calling.

Many caregivers discover their calling early. They know as soon as they begin serving the needs of others that they were meant to do that kind of work. One thing caregivers need never wonder about is whether their efforts make a difference, for the needs they serve are significant.

Yet many caregivers are surprised at how good they feel when they choose to make a personal sacrifice to help another. What is that strange feeling we experience (if we're open to it) when we give love? I often hear people say things like, "I interrupted my day to help walk someone to their car in the parking lot. At first I was thinking, 'What a pain in the neck.' Instead, I found that I felt wonderful for quite a while afterwards."

I believe that good feeling comes because giving puts us in alignment with love's energy. When we give love, God's light flashes through us.

For people who choose to make caregiving their calling, that light can stream through them every day, even on occasions when they're beginning to feel exhausted. For this to happen, caregivers may need to reshape how they think about work. If caregiving is a job, the light will rarely come. If

caregiving is a calling, the light will come to them whenever they are *present* to it.

Not everyone is comfortable with thinking of their work as a calling. For some, the word "calling" may awaken uncomfortable feelings (for them) about religion.

The Loving Care Movement invites people to think about caregiving as the alignment of their best human energy with love's energy. The first step in this process is for us to recognize *the sacred nature* of caregiving work.

Caregiving often involves a potentially intimate exchange with a patient or client. This is because of the deep vulnerability of people in need. The vulnerable bring their deep need to us asking for help. This need may be everything from cancer to childbirth to instances of abuse.

Caregivers can rob these encounters of their sacredness by treating the encounter as a routine transaction. This kind of thinking is what causes some nurses, technologists, physicians, and other caregivers to fail miserably in their communication.

I remember dealing with one patient who complained about abusive treatment from her physician.

"What did he do?" I asked the patient.

"I was waiting anxiously in the recovery room for the results of my breast biopsy," she said. "My doctor walked out of the O.R. and right past me. Then, almost as if it was an afterthought, he stopped, then called over the heads of three other patients: 'By the way, you've got cancer.' Then he just walked away."

Most of us in healthcare are familiar with stories like this. When I spoke with this surgeon (a former Marine who fancied himself a medical version of John Wayne), it was clear to me that he was caught up in the definition of his work as a job filled with tasks. He had trouble understanding why his encounter had been hurtful. He said something like, "How I deliver the news doesn't *change* the news does it, Erie? What am I supposed to do, hold her hand?"

Of course, the answer to this might well have been yes. But I didn't say this, because this doctor, at that moment in his life, could not have engaged in an encounter like that with sincerity.

Then something terrible happened to him.

Less than six months after that incident, this surgeon's daughter was killed in a snowmobile accident. When I saw him at the funeral home, it was clear he had changed. As soon as I looked into his eyes, I knew he was recalling our conversation: "All the officer said to me was, 'Your daughter's dead,'" he told me with tears in his eyes. And I knew he meant that the officer had reported the information the way he had spoken to his patient—as if the officer thought of his daughter as an animal that had been struck by a falling tree.

I wish I could tell you that this physician went on to become one of the most compassionate surgeons I ever met. Instead, he quit practice soon after the tragedy. I was surprised and touched to learn that after a few months of retirement, he put his suturing skills to work—as a seamstress in his wife's dressmaking shop! Perhaps this was his true calling, these were his sealed orders. In any case, his transformation told me something we all need to recall—there is often a kind and gentle soul beneath the brusque exterior we encounter. The challenge of the Loving Care Movement is to awaken that gentle soul and put it into balance with the strength we also need to be effective.

When we open our sealed orders and live our calling as caregivers, it is so much easier for us to be present to those we encounter. A life of calling is a life energized by passion. Called caregivers are easy to distinguish from average caregivers. You can identify them by the extraordinary effort they put into their work unaffected by whether they have a good supervisor or a bad one, or whether they are working in a short-staffed situation or a fully staffed environment.

Called caregivers travel through life with a special blessing. They live with the light of love in their hearts. It shows through their eyes, in the way they touch people, in the grace with which they live. It doesn't always come automatically. Called caregivers, like anyone else, have their bad days. But in their darkest moments, they remember that their work has meaning. This hope invariably drives away the shadows.

If we're not feeling energized in our work, it's time to stop blaming the person we report to. We all report to patients, not to a boss. If we're feeling beaten down in our work, it may well be because we are seeing our role as a job, not a calling. As you meditate, seek to open the way to ask if you are in the right work; if you are a called caregiver, rejoice in the light of love.

When we are present to our calling, we are present to our lives. Unseal your orders from God.

Love's Fifth Principle

Follow Guiding Principles, Not Rules

Rules are for robots. Principles are for people.

—E.C.

Love's Fifth Principle is *about* principles. Perhaps it should be the first principle since it describes why principles need to be our guiding lights along the pathway of caregiving.

So often, people look around for rules to guide them in their lives. But the world is too complex to live by rules. The more we live by rules, the less we are living our humanity. Rules call for rote behavior. Principles require thinking.

After thirty years in healthcare, I'm acutely aware of the rules-consciousness of hospitals and the government. As a lawyer, I'm also aware that every rule requires interpretation—something only a human being can do. What are the guiding principles in your life?

You know that my first guiding principle is to *Live Love, Not Fear.* I believe that we need principles like this to remind us that the most important thing we can do is to give to others. Here is one of my favorite principles: "In order to accomplish anything important, we must love it more than our own ease."

This was written by George Eliot, the female author of *Silas Marner* and *Middlemarch*, who took a man's name because it was so difficult for women to publish their novels in the 19th century. Eliot herself, as a member of the English gentry, could have elected a life of ease and comfort. Instead she embarked on the path to become a writer, and by the end of the 19th century was considered one of the greatest novelists in English history.

Living love is so difficult a goal that it illustrates why we must love this goal more than our own ease. It's an odd combination of words. We must love Love (giving to others) in order to escape the boundaries of our own comfort. And this is exactly why the principle of Love is such an important guide.

The wisdom of loving principles goes back at least to Aristotle, who wrote that "the wicked obey from fear and the good from love." Rules are the shield used by bureaucrats who have neither the wisdom nor the courage to act on their own. These are the people who explain mean-spirited behavior by saying, "Hey, I'm just following the rules."

How do we know when and how to follow a given rule? For true lovers, the answer will always be found in the heart, not in the rulebook.

Love's Sixth Principle

Take Your Work Seriously, Not Yourself

Take your work seriously, not yourself.

— Senator Robert Kennedy

W e're all vulnerable to this hazard. We go through lots of education and training and one day we arrive in the role of caregiver. We are entrusted with the care of another. It's a big responsibility and carries with it a measure of power. Soon we may fall victim to thinking our work is so important that *we* must be also. This leads to the condition reflected in the line above. We begin taking ourselves seriously as well as our work. In the middle of grim times, we may lose balance.

If the condition really gets out of hand, we may fall victim to some version of the "God complex." In this state, we think we are more important than anyone else. It's pretty hard to remember we're one of the grains of sand if we subconsciously think we're big shots.

I first heard the line about not taking ourselves as seriously as our work from the late Senator Robert F. Kennedy. I think Kennedy quoted the line because he knew that at times in his own career he had fallen victim to taking himself too seriously. He seemed to do this during both the McCarthy and the Hoffa hearings in the 1950s.

By the time his brother became President, he seemed to have a better sense of self-deprecating humor. Perhaps some of his brother's own keen wit rubbed off on Bobby. Instead of being embarrassed about the idea of appointing his own brother as Attorney General in 1961, President Kennedy joked that he had considered making the announcement by peeking out of the door at 2 a.m. and whispering, "It's Bobby."

Another great illustration of JFK's self-deprecating humor is reflected in his response to a teenager who asked him, during the presidential campaign of 1960, how he became a hero. If Kennedy had taken himself very seriously, he might have launched into a story about his heroism after the sinking of the PT boat he commanded. Instead, he simply said, "It was involuntary. They sank my boat."

Similarly, at a $100-a-plate luncheon Kennedy said, "I could say I'm deeply touched. But not as deeply touched as you have been in coming to this luncheon."

Abe Lincoln, arguably our greatest president, was famous for his wit, as demonstrated in this light comment at the opening to one of his speeches. "I have stepped out upon this platform that I may see you and that you may see me, and in the arrangement I have the best of the bargain."

Lincoln is also the man who said: "Nearly all men can stand adversity, but if you want to test a man's character, give him power." And that is part of the point of this sixth principle. Humor helps keep us in balance. Self-deprecating humor, along with our own willingness to accept jokes about ourselves, is one of the great ways of retaining humility.

Caregiving work can be grim. Retaining our sense of humor has a way of keeping us humble, and of helping us stay balanced so that we can give our best energy to people in need. It's awfully hard to laugh and be angry at the same time. And humor is one of the best weapons against frustration and burnout.

If you think you've been taking yourself seriously as well as your work, consider the wisdom of this principle. Begin practicing it by trying out jokes about yourself *on* yourself.

All of us have funny truths about us, don't we? In my own case, for example, my hair is thinning so rapidly I don't need a hair dryer anymore. All I do is ask my wife to blow on my wet hair a couple times and it's dry.

Love's Seventh Principle

Live in Gratitude

Gratitude is not only the greatest of virtues, but the parent of all the others.

— Cicero

I s gratitude truly the parent of all the other virtues as Cicero wrote more than two thousand years ago? The more I think about it, the more I agree that it is. Gratitude is a beautiful form of self-care. When we live in its glow, we feel love's light passing through us. This gives us the strength to practice some of the other virtues.

It also helps free us from some of life's vices. As I cultivate gratitude, anger eases away from me, frustration departs, hunger for approval eases.

In gratitude, I feel blessed. In this state, I am all the more likely to want to give to others, to reach out to the poor, to help the vulnerable. For gratitude is not the same as complacency. Complacency is a form of arrogance. When I am grateful, I seek to share more with others.

President Kennedy said, *"We must never forget that the highest appreciation is not to utter words, but to live by them."* This is why gratitude is such a crucial practice for caregivers. As appreciation flows through us for our many blessings, we want to be a blessing to those who are less fortunate. We want to live the words we speak.

As with the other six principles, the practice of gratitude can be difficult. We are more likely to make a list of our problems than a list of our blessings. This is what Eric Hoffer understood when he wrote, *"The hardest arithmetic to master is that which enables us to count our blessings."*

We need to make counting our blessings a ritual of thoughtfulness because each time we do this we are refreshed with love. The author of *Proverbs* wrote, *He who refreshes others will himself be refreshed.*11:25 This tells us that as we share the blessing of our love with others, we will find a further refreshment.

This practice does not mean a continual pattern of comparison with others' travails. The practice of gratitude is not enhanced with language like, "I'm so glad I don't have cancer like Gladys does." This is an ineffective practice of love because this language can cause us to look down on Gladys with pity. In order to elevate ourselves, we unwittingly step on

the shoulders of another who we may imagine is worse off than (or below) us.

Instead, we can revel in whatever good health, good fortune, or joy we may have. In the process, we will be living by the seventh principle and discovering, as with each of the other six principles, that living love is living with joy.

As Meister Eckhart spoke: "If the only prayer you said in your whole life was, 'thank you,' that would suffice."

THREE LIFE-CHANGING RITUALS FOR THE SPIRIT

Consider how three rituals can change your life.

- *Ritual #1,* the **Three-Second Pause**, is the across-the-day reminder of the humanity of the other person. Practice it and you will deepen your own humanity.

- *Ritual #2,* a **Three-Minute Reading** of a meditation, introduces the practice of mindfulness and thoughtful reflection into your life.

- *Ritual #3* is **Five-Minute Magic**. This five- (or twenty-) minute meditation helps you stay centered from within rather than reacting entirely to the noise of the outside world.

Added together, these practices can take less than ten minutes in your day. Engage in this trio of practices and you will feel your life changing for the better.

Ritual for the Spirit #1

The Three-Second Pause

Anurse pauses three seconds before entering one of her patient's rooms, repeats to herself, "This is a person made vulnerable by illness." She then enters the room with grace and an open heart, ready to respond to the needs of a suffering human being.

This nurse's pause at the door reflects a lovely if uncommon ritual, taught in some nursing schools and practiced infrequently. Before entering a patient's room, remember the special nature of caregiving. Recall the essential humanity of the person in need.

What if each of us engaged in a similar kind of ritual before every encounter with another (and mid-encounter)? Why is such a reminder necessary?

Amid the hectic demands of caregiving, it can be hard to remember, much less practice, such a fine ritual. There are challenging obstacles.

1. Some patients are disoriented and confused. If you're assigned to care for patients suffering from dementia, it may take a special effort to recall the equal humanity of the person.

2. Some patients are unconscious. If you're an operating or recovery room caregiver, it may take special sensitivity to treat the inanimate form in front of you with the respect each human deserves.

3. Some patients are rude and inconsiderate. It always challenges a caregiver to be compassionate toward a patient who is shouting in your face.

4. Caregiving work has elements of the routine. The repetitiveness of certain caregiving duties may dull or harden the sensitivity of some towards others.

Imagine the impact if every caregiver engaged in the three-second ritual several times each day. I don't mean only nurses, but *every* technologist, housekeeper, dietician, information tech, maintenance worker, and, by golly, every executive as well! This simple three-second pause could trans-

form the delivery of compassionate care in America because it reinforces what has been lost in so many organizations: mindfulness.

Another small practice I instituted as CEO at Baptist Hospital in Nashville was to call upon all caregivers to knock before entering. Even this little courtesy is ignored in most hospitals. The door knock announces, respectfully, your arrival. As if the patient room is the patient's bedroom, not a public lobby. The three-second pause reminds caregivers of the sacred nature of their work.

If you've ever been a patient, you know how much you may feel like a hostage. You lie there disabled and dressed in a terrible garment called a patient gown. Naturally, you would prefer the privacy of your own bedroom or at least the relative sanctity of a hotel room. Instead, a vast array of strangers enter and leave your room as if there were no door at all.

How can we restore "the sacred" to caregiving? The three-second pause,

ritualized into daily and nightly practice and accompanied by taking a breath, is a good start. It could go a long way toward helping not only patients, but caregivers. Each three seconds blesses the special nature of caregiving. Each three-second hesitation increases the chance that the patient will be treated with love. Each three-second reflection becomes a sort of mini-meditation for each caregiver, allowing more of a chance for love's grace to shine through.

REFLECTIVE PRACTICE

- Imagine a sentence or two you could say to yourself in your own three-second ritual. It can be something like: *This is person before me is a child of God, or a child of love.* If you would prefer something less religious, consider: *I am healthy and privileged to be able to care for this person in need.*

- The language doesn't have to be the same every time since we don't want the thought to be too automatic or mechanical. It is the pausing that is ritualized. The thought should be consciously compassionate and should be accompanied by taking a breath.

- Start this practice *today* and continue it every day from now on.

Ritual for the Spirit #2

Three-Minute Reading

For leaders and many caregivers, organizational life turns heavily on a strange rhythm of gatherings called meetings. Nobody admits they like meetings and everybody says they want less of them. Having attended thousands, I can often see why many people dread them. Meetings can raise energy, but most meetings drain it away. No one wants more meetings. Everyone would like more meaningful meetings—gatherings in which the mission of loving care is truly advanced.

Most faith-based, and some other, organizations begin meetings with a brief devotional. It usually takes a few minutes after which the leader will often say something like: "Now let's get down to business." The brief devotional is tossed aside by most as a necessary evil rather than a true source of inspiration to inform the texture of the rest of the meeting. This can change if leaders and team members find the courage to make a few changes. A daily meditation may take *less than three minutes* to read.

In fact, many meditations are written to be read in a few minutes with the hope that the reader will reflect awhile longer and absorb the reflection into their being. Our spirits must be fed as well as our minds and bodies. When caregiver spirits are not refreshed with reflection, burnout can settle in.

Meditations remind us of the meaning of our daily endeavors. A key sign of burnout is a loss of meaning in our work.

Each day we ask others how they are doing. An equally important question is: How are you *being*?

Three minutes reading a meditation—here in this book or from some other source—can help support caregivers who are seeking to be present to life. That is a principle goal of meditation—to help you in *your* goal to be present—to help you breathe in meaning and breathe out love.

Ritual #2 calls us to set aside time for a Three-Minute Reading and three more minutes to reflect. We need to quiet ourselves at different moments across the day because it is in the quiet space that we can reconnect with love's light.

Take a few minutes now, to pause, breathe, and reflect. I know you're busy. I also know you would like to breathe more life into your days. Three minutes reading a meditation can help you find your breath and your heart.

Ritual for the Spirit #3

Five-Minute Magic

Meditation is being mainlined by the mainstream, from corporate offices to factory floors.

—Eve Savory, reporter, *CBC News* (Canada)

Michael Herman, a senior partner with the law firm of Goodman and Goodman, meditates in his office on a regular basis. Saint Joseph's hospital in Toronto offers meditation courses for staff, and nearly four hundred caregivers take advantage of the training every year.

What's going on? How can busy lawyers and caregivers jump off the roller-coaster of work demands long enough to do what some consider to be "nothing"?

The answer is something Buddhists discovered twenty-five centuries ago in one part of the world, Jewish rabbis learned even further back in another part of the world, Hindus learned in a third way, and Christians and Moslems learned later. Meditation is a critical element of spiritual living.

As I travel the country speaking to groups in hospitals and charities, I ask about self-care. Uniformly, everyone thinks it's important—and, simultaneously, most American caregivers say they are doing a lousy job of it.

In order to care for others, we must first care for ourselves. "How many people take twenty minutes a day in meditation?" I ask. Rarely, a hand will go up. "How many are taking five minutes a day?" A few more hands (in a crowd of a hundred) will go up. The rest of the group sits with their hands in their lap. They have been unable or, more likely, are unwilling to find five minutes.

Not setting aside that precious time means that life has got these people by the throat. The ten-minute break in many workplaces is still, to a remarkable degree, smoke- and noise-filled instead of informed by silence.

Work culture can change that. Ritual #3 calls caregivers to take just five minutes once a day to sit with their eyes closed and attend to their breathing. This is not nap time, this is meditation time. If you've never done this, all you have to know is how to sit upright in a regular chair, hands in lap, eyes closed. The way to deal with anxious thoughts is to replace them with a positive sound or restful word or simply to listen to your breath. The way to avoid worrying if the time is up is to take a glance at your watch and then let go. You'll know when the time has passed. The way to free yourself of distracting noise is to let it go by.

The sole goal of Ritual #3 is stunningly simple—sitting with your eyes closed for five to twenty minutes. Over ninety percent of the people with whom I do this exercise report feeling refreshed and energized after this five-minute "vacation." This refreshment can last for more than an hour afterwards. For those wise enough to take a full twenty minutes in meditation, extensive studies show that the positive results last six to eight hours!

It's hard to change patterns. Twenty minutes is required for a fuller meditation experience. But five minutes, a sort of mini-meditation, will help—especially if you touch some peaceful center that you can tap into across the day.

Maybe you can find a work partner who will support you in your mini-meditation practice and the two of you can go to the hospital chapel, an office, or, weather permitting, outdoors. In the same way people exercise together, perhaps you and your partner can help each other rest together.

Meditations, short or long, are an essential element in self-care. Ritual #3, the five-minute (or twenty-minute) ritual, is virtually guaranteed to improve your life. Whether you choose to do it is, of course, in your hands. But know this. As Ms. Savory reports: *"Meditation is now out of the closet. The word is, it eases stress, drops blood pressure, helps put that bad day at the office in perspective."*

Wise caregivers will not only give it a try, they will make it a part of their day, *every* day.

REFLECTIONS ON LOVING

TOMB OF THE UNKNOWN CAREGIVER

We know them. Yet they are not seen or remembered by name. They are the legions of loving caregivers who tended our ancestors, gave their compassion and their skill to strangers, lived with the golden thread of healing in their hands.

From 1893 to 1926 she rose most days at dawn, neatened her thousand-threaded hair, drew her uniform about her, slipped her feet into quiet shoes, came to care for your great-grandfather and the other ten men in the ward, helping them to rise, spooning porridge into their mouths, sponging their weathered backs.

From 1926 to 1949, he worked the night shift, mopping the linoleum floors of the hospital that has since been torn down, raking dirt beneath incandescence, smiling to those among the sick who saw him.

Each day and night, from July 2, 1863 to July 7, 1863, beneath the steaming canvas, amid the stench of blood and death, she laid wetted towels on the faces of fallen soldiers as surgeons sawed off their legs and cut away their arms. Later, she read the Bible to the newly blind, sang soft into their fear, smiled.

Just before nightfall, November 12, 1738, he opened the door of Hotel Dieu de Paris to yet another man in rags, helped him across the threshold to an open place on the floor, gave him water, fed him, held his hand.

On the night of January 5th, 1950, he wrapped chains around the tires of his black Plymouth, drove it across snow-slick Wisconsin roads, entered a weathered farmhouse, washed his hands twice, guided triplets out of their mother and into their first home. Lacking an incubator, he laid them on a blanket on the open door of the oven, tended them and their mother until dawn when he drove off to his office of waiting patients.

After the priest passed by and the Levite turned his back, the Samaritan knelt to tend the pain of the wounded stranger by the road, lifted him aboard his animal, led him to an inn, paid for his care.

A month after she was laid off as a nurse's aide, no one could remember her name. A day after he retired, his name badge was recycled. After the nursing home closed, she who cared for others lived but six more months, dying alone in her sleep.

Tonight, all these spirits walk the halls of hospitals, hospices, nursing homes. They stand at bedsides in rural shacks where pain needs healing, whisper to us to feed the homeless, touch the "untouchable," love the "unlovable."

They are the unknown caregivers who once held the golden thread of healing in their hands. They have no tomb. No place to rest but heaven. One day, we who hold the golden thread may join them.

OUR BETTER ANGELS

We are not enemies, but friends. We must not be enemies...The mystic chords of memory...will yet swell the chorus... when again touched... by the better angels of our nature.

—Abraham Lincoln,
First Inaugural Address, March 4, 1861

One of Disney's classic cartoons portrays the friendly old dog Goofy in a quandary. A cat has fallen down a well and calls out to be saved. The dog rubs his chin, unsure what to do next. At this moment "the better angel of his nature" appears on his right shoulder. "Save the cat," the kind angel pleads. Goofy begins pulling on a rope to lift the cat to safety.

But a second angel, holding a pitchfork, appears on Goofy's left shoulder: "Let the cat *drown*, Goofy. You're a dog, that's a cat. Dogs don't save cats." Confused, Goofy lets go of the rope and the cat falls back into the well. The angel argument rages back and forth as Goofy alternately raises the cat, lowers him, then raises him again.

Watching this movie in the Bruin Theater at age six, I thought the choice was clear. Goofy should save the cat. I cheered for the better angel on his right shoulder and wondered why Goofy seemed uncertain what to do. A few rows behind me, the voices of three older boys gave me an answer. "Let the cat drown, you dumb dog," they shouted.

The simple circumstance of this cartoon makes choice look easy to some. More complex choices may leave us as immobilized as Goofy. If the cat down the well is my enemy, why should I save him? If I do, he'll just continue to bedevil me. On the other hand, I believe in kindness, in helping others, in life, so I must save another in distress.

If people always chose their better angels, most of the human problems of the world would vanish. For Lincoln, in 1861, the choice was clear. He called his southern brethren, and all Americans, to listen to their better angels, stay with the Union, avoid war. Many heard other voices. Hundreds of thousands of people suffered and died because of those who refused to heed Lincoln's appeal.

Our lives are flooded with the voices of many more than just two angels. Perhaps you have some of the same aggravating ones that I do.

Lazy Angel: This angel sits all day in an easy chair, raising only enough energy to shout to me that I should quit trying so hard. At this very moment, he advises me to stop writing, lie down, turn on the television, take a nap. Every so often, I listen to him because sometimes he's right. It's good to rest. Other times, he is masquerading as the voice of despair. He tells me to give up because nothing I do matters anyway. "You can't change things," he calls out from his easy chair, "give up and rest."

Proud Angel: This is the angel who wants me to win credit for any good thing I do. "Get your name up in lights," this angel calls. "Be famous, win applause, cover yourself in glory." This angel is fed by praise and suffers when unheard.

Greedy Angel: A close friend of the Proud Angel, this fellow is hungry for money, food, new things. He is lavish in his desires for me and stingy toward those who want anything from me. When charity seeks my help, he shouts, "Save your money. Don't spare a dime. Use it instead to buy something for yourself."

Shaming Angel: This devil with a pitchfork tells me I'm no good and never will be. When I do something wrong, he smiles with delight. "I told you you're a sinner. Thanks for proving me right."

There are many more angels like this quartet. And there are plenty of kind ones who call for the best in me. We sit amidst this chorus wishing the mean ones would fall silent so we may hear the songs of the better ones. Meditation helps us find this silence and within it, the strength we need *to find balance.*

EXERCISE

Sit, close your eyes, take a five-minute vacation at least twice a day or, even better, make it a full twenty minutes. Meditation always enhances life experience, improves our analytical skills, opens us to the voices of Love, Truth, and Beauty.

ON FAKING COMPASSION

The intuitive mind is a sacred gift and the rational mind is a faithful servant.
We have created a society that honors the servant and has forgotten the gift.

—Albert Einstein

The internist sitting next to me in the doctor's dining room at Nashville's Baptist Hospital appeared to be in her mid-thirties. "How do you give loving care?" I asked.

"I'm an actress," she replied. "I start rounds before seven. Mostly, I pretend to care. If I gave compassion to all my patients, I'd be exhausted by noon."

Any psychologist knows that maintaining a great distance between our behavior and who we really are requires great effort. After awhile, faking can lead to burnout. The genuine expression of compassion, on the other hand, may sometimes feel painful, yet each compassionate act reinforces a caregiver's humanity.

Faking compassion demeans caregiver as well as patient. Pretending to be kind, as this doctor feels she needs to do, requires a depleting kind of energy. While she pretends compassion, what is going on in her heart? Is she silently counting the seconds until she can escape to her charts? Is she resenting the person before her? Is she simply engaged in an innocent act of trying to protect herself from pain? Or has she never learned to express compassion?

Keith Hagan, M.D., is one of the most compassionate and capable physicians I know. When I told him the above story, he shook his head in sadness. I could see that his great heart felt badly for a physician who had not yet learned that compassion is a gift to the giver as well as the patient.

Another genius at expressing compassion is Mel Davis, M.D. An oncologist (now with the Cleveland Clinic), he cared for cancer patients at Riverside Methodist Hospital in Columbus during the 1980s and '90s when I served there as President. No matter what time of day or night I did administrative rounds, Dr. Davis was always there, sitting with his patients, comforting their families, casting his soft eyes on the caregivers with whom he worked.

Another oncologist in the same hospital took a different view. As soon as his patients moved beyond the chance of a successful cure, he would withdraw. On occasion, families complained to me that this physician had abandoned his patient. I would often call on Dr. Davis, and with his angelic grace, he would step in to help.

Why do we feel that compassion is like a pitcher of water, each pour a dose leaving less water behind? For doctors like Keith Hagan and Mel Davis, compassion is an artesian well—an ever-flowing stream that replenishes itself.

This doesn't mean that saints don't get tired. It means that they know that the intuitive mind, as Einstein said, is a sacred gift. With rest, the fountain of compassion will flow again. For it is as endless as God's love.

MEDITATION ON OUR LEGACY

I ain't dead yet.

—Woody Guthrie

We express ourselves in our work, whether we want to our not. Our legacy of spirit is not something aimed at a history book but is something that arrows through each of us each day and enters the hearts of others.

History doesn't feel our love. People do.

We fill/spill our library of tears, shake our rattles full of laughter, tip our cups of anger, needle out our frustration, offer our gifts of compassion, and it's all there in our work.

The surprise is, it turns out that everything matters.

And since everything matters, then you matter and I matter and the nurse bringing you a styrofoam cup of cool water to still your thirst matters, because you need and she is needed.

All the love in the world will meet some of the need, bathe this need in her soft eyes, salve it with finger strokes, cool pain's fire with the breeze of her breath.

You have loved and given love. You have suffered and carry scars.

Since everything matters, what will you do today to love away another's need? Will you leave work one night, on your last night, with your love unspent—circling unused in the jungle of your fear?

Will you leave work one day, at the end of your last day, knowing you have spread the cloak of your compassion to stanch the fire of another's agony?

What legacy will you celebrate at the end of this day? The one you are living now? It's the only one you will ever have.

EXPLOSIONS AND EPIPHANIES

There's not much news in poems. But men die every day for lack of what is found there.

—William Carlos Williams

It was July 4,1950. I was six years old when Dad told me to stand back as he put a little tube with a string sprouting from it under an empty Campbell's soup can. He lit the wick and shouted: "Cover your ears."

The firecracker exploded. The soup can rocketed above my head. As soon as gravity returned the can to earth, I begged, "Lemme light one, lemme light one, huh, Dad?" But no, I wasn't old enough yet.

I'm more than old enough now, but I haven't lit a firecracker since I was eleven or twelve. The explosions that interest me now are the epiphanies of spring when yellow explodes along the arms of forsythia and an eternal purple shines through time amid once gray-brown woods.

And there are those dazzling bursts of light that happen each day and night when caregivers reach out to ease pain, help mothers in labor, or hold the hands of people on the edge of death.

I am enchanted by the quiet epiphanies that occur in the hearts of those who suddenly discover a kind of beauty and truth to which they had previously been blind.

One of my favorite phrases is: *Where attention goes, energy flows.* Exploding firecrackers release energy into the air with blasts of light and ear-perforating sound. They catch our attention for a moment, then vanish. Unless, of course, we are traumatized by the event, lose a finger or an eye, and spend the rest of our lives focusing our energy on the day of our loss rather than any gains that happened in the meantime.

History's eye focuses on the firecracker events that explode inside epochs. The attention-getting eras of the twentieth century are its two world wars. Peace is so much less interesting to the mostly male authors of our history books.

The same is true of the local news. Fights and controversy command attention. The weatherperson seems thrilled to report impending storms and vaguely disappointed if the skies are clear and calm.

What events have exploded within your life—creating earthquake shifts in your world view? What amount of your life has been spent mourning losses compared with aiming your attention toward celebrating joy?

The head of a local charity told me her father was murdered when she was nine. How do you recover from that kind of explosion? In her case, more explosions followed—her mother remarried, to a man who was a drug dealer and abusive. He ended up in prison. She and her mother struggled to live in the jaws of poverty, but there was little help available for the innocent families of people in prison.

One day this woman experienced a different kind of explosion—a true epiphany that changed her life. She decided to move her attention away from her losses and to celebrate what she could do to help others. Who would help the families of prisoners? She decided to take on this challenge herself, choosing to focus her attention on leading a charity that would support the other silent victims of crime—the children of prisoners.

Once she gave her life to loving others, she became flooded with love herself. As a young girl, she was shattered by a series of explosions herself. She could have used her life tragedies as a justification to drown in alcohol and drugs—to turn her back on life. Instead, she found the wisdom and courage to be present to her life and to the needs of others. She learned to convert the *de*structive power of her tragedies into a *con*structive ministry to the innocent families of imprisoned men and women. She lives in love and gratitude instead of bitterness and hate.

The news doesn't report such energy shifts from negative to positive. There's not much news in the poetry of epiphany. But there is meaning that can inform our lives with each day and night—enabling us to notice the light within us and turn toward it. Tonight, beyond the fireworks bursting above the heads of crowds, many individual caregivers will be lending the strength of their hearts and hands to the many who have been weakened by illness and who would otherwise be alone. Bless these caregivers with your prayers, for their work is solitary and exhausting.

And as you journey through your time on this earth, think of ways you can redirect your energy so that your presence enriches the lives of others. *Where attention goes, energy flows. Change your attention and you change your life.*

REFLECTION

*Behind the fireworks of this day hides
our personal epiphany.
The purple/red/yellow gleam flashing
against black is a mirror reflecting
back to your heart its own rainbow of
colors. Your beauty and grace have
always been within. You are a child of
God. Celebrate your inner light
and it will shine through your eyes
illuminating the lives of others as
they wonder at how much better they
feel in the glow of your presence.*

EXPECTATION AND HOPE

O ne of the great obstacles to serenity in life is our human inclination to create expectations for things beyond our control. Why won't the weather cooperate? Why won't my fellow caregiver work as hard as I do? Why doesn't my team win as much as I expected? Expectations are natural. Yet they can generate frustrations and steal precious time from the Lake of Now.

What is the difference between expectations and hope? To expect is to project a desire on another thing or person or event. Hope is a belief (not an expectation) that things will turn out for the best.

Television host, author, speaker, and longtime family friend Art Linkletter may seem like an unlikely philosopher to turn to. Yet his long life (he's 93 and still speaking around the country) is a triumph of hope. Linkletter offers a useful phrase for today's meditation: "Things turn out best for people who make the best of the way things turn out." If life doesn't meet your expectations, find ways to sustain hope in the midst of your now.

These things are easy to say and hard to live. Dr. Viktor Frankl is the leading exponent of the notion that he or she who has a why, can survive any how. His counsel can be helpful to beleaguered caregivers who, in the midst of compassion fatigue, may have trouble living in the present. Is the why in your life big enough to help you survive the difficult moments?

Many of us know the Serenity Prayer of Reinhold Niebuhr, but most of us only know the first lines and think of them as designed for alcoholics, not for us. But his language can help every caregiver.

> *God grant me the serenity*
> *to accept the things I cannot change;*
> *courage to change the things I can;*
> *and wisdom to know the difference.*

Here's the rest of Niebuhr's brilliant prayer:

> *Living one day at a time;*
> *Enjoying one moment at a time;*
> *Accepting hardships as the pathway to peace;*
> *Taking, as He did, this sinful world*
> *as it is, not as I would have it;*

Trusting that He will make all things right
if I surrender to His Will;
That I may be reasonably happy in this life
and supremely happy with Him
Forever in the next. Amen.

But my favorite words on hope were written by Emily Dickinson in her poem that begins:

Hope is the thing with feathers
That perches in the soul,
And sings the tune—without the words,
And never stops at all...

To help me deal with the notion of expectations, I made my own effort at writing a meditation that I hope will help you as it did me:

Expectations

Give up
your expectations
for the world.
Skies, indifferent to your wishes, will cloud.

Give up expecting the sun as if it would
shine to meet your expectations.

Give up
your expectations
for others.
Does it help for you to suppose others
will fit the mold you have crafted for them?
Embrace them now as they are and they become
someone to love.

Surrender
your expectations
for victory.

Your hand-wringing from the stands will
not turn the tide. God doesn't care who wins.

Live
in the now
of defeat as well as triumph.
Expectations are a straight jacket.
Hope has feathers.
Now is the rhythm of your breath.

—E.C.

EXERCISE

Watch your thoughts today and become aware of how much of your life is built around expectations about others. How much of your frustration in life comes from people not meeting expectations you have set for them?

Start your five-minute or twenty-minute meditation with a reflection on the hope in your life. At the end of your meditation, resolve to live in the now, no matter what that now holds.

Let go of expectations. Cultivate hope. Live love in your now.

WHEN FORGIVING CAREGIVER ERRORS IS WISE AS WELL AS LOVING

Love's One-Liner: We are not our mistakes, we are children of God who err.

When French soccer star Zinadine Zidane head-butted an opponent in the World Championship on July 9, 2006, and was ejected, it was clear that millions would pass harsh judgment on this now hapless hero. In an instant, the great Zidane jeopardized his legacy as one of the finest players in the history of the world's most popular sport. When Italy went on to win, the hostility toward Zidane intensified. Announcers and other commentators heaped venom on this man's "shameful act." The hero of France had, in the eyes of many, suddenly become a goat. Would he, should he, will he, ever be forgiven?

Indeed, are any of us truly forgiven for our misdeeds—intended or accidental? Most of us ignore the long legacy of religious and other spiritual teaching about withholding judgment and extending forgiveness. We are quick to cast blame. "What a fool, what an idiot, how unforgivable," we huff when someone else makes a mistake.

Putting aside the history of highly visible sports gaffs (Bill Buckner of the Red Sox comes to mind for his innocent, but fatal-to-victory, muff of a ground ball in the 1986 World Series), the real question becomes: why is it so hard for us to forgive?

Doctors and nurses are often sued for their mistakes as if money could somehow create healing. But the pain for these caregivers is often not measured in money but in the quantity of shame and harsh judgments of others, not to mention the calumny they heap on themselves.

And that is part of the problem with forgiveness. It's the difference between responsibility and shame—between holding people accountable and damning them as sinners. Forgiveness does not mean an instant endorsement of a bad choice. It does mean condemning the act and forgiving the person.

Caregivers are fired every day, sometimes justifiably, for mistakes that jeopardize the safety and well-being of others. There is an important dis-

tinction, however, between chronic mistakes and the rare error made by an otherwise qualified caregiver. And there is an even more important difference between the act of making a mistake and the person. We are not our mistakes and neither is anybody else.

One day, during the time I was President and CEO of a hospital system, the news came of a serious mistake in the Central Services Department. A technician missed one of the steps during the instrument sterilization cycle. As a result there was a chance that up to thirty patients had been operated on by instruments less than completely clean.

Instantly, steps were initiated to assure the safety of each of these patients and to protect against infection. I also asked that each patient, through their doctor, be told of the hospital's mistake and that the hospital would take full responsibility.

But what about the technician? "Fire him," some said instantly. But several things stopped me from taking this action.

The technician had a long and exemplary record of reliability and excellent performance. In fact, it was he who had noticed his error and reported it.

The technician was horrified by his own mistake and deeply remorseful.

My sense was that this incident was likely to make him *more* reliable in the future. Most conscientious people become more careful, not less, after a serious mistake.

Some may have thought I was wrong to block termination of this employee. But I wanted to make a point. We all make errors. If they're rare, we're entitled to forgiveness and the chance to keep our jobs. If they're common, we lose our jobs, but we're still, all of us, entitled to be treated with respect because it is human to err. Further, we want to encourage honest and prompt reporting, not punish it and thereby frighten others into silence. Loving care is about trust, openness, forgiveness.

I talked with my daughter about this. She was in her second year at Harvard at the time. "The Greeks built flaws into their heroes," she reminded me. "Why do we insist on perfection?" Yes, Achilles had his vulnerable heel. And the Greeks were, in so many ways, wiser than we are today. Still, so many faith traditions preach forgiveness. I think one of the main reasons it's hard to forgive is that blaming someone else always makes it easier on *us*. If someone else is at fault, then *we* don't have to carry the crushing burden of responsibility, do we?

If I'm engaged in a pattern of irritability and disrespect toward others, and can keep blaming them for my behavior, then I don't have to take responsibility for making changes in myself. If I can blame you, then I don't have to face all the hard work I need to do to transform me.

So Frenchmen turn their ire on Zidane because it's so painful to lose. They want him to shoulder at least part of the pain, whether he deserves it or not.

It probably helped the circumstance of the Central Service technician that no patients became ill. But I like to think he would be forgiven anyway. I can tell you that, so grateful was he not to be fired, he became an even more exemplary employee after this incident and, last time I checked, was still working at the hospital.

Everyone in an organization watches how errors are treated. Chronic mistakes are unacceptable because they risk patient safety. Isolated errors can provide a special opportunity for leaders to show the human side of a healing culture—to demonstrate both respect, wisdom, and the most valuable of all leadership characteristics: love.

THE PRACTICE OF FORGIVENESS

■ It begins in the mirror. If we can't forgive ourselves, how can we forgive others?

■ Separate the act from the actor. We are not our mistakes. We are children of God.

■ Forgiveness is not the same as approval. Forgiveness is not about approving negative behavior. It's about accepting the person, not accepting mistakes.

■ Stop recording mistakes as if they were a list of sins to be stored up for later recounting. Take on responsibility, not shame.

■ Practice forgiveness by extending it to someone you don't think deserves it.

THE CAREGIVER'S SURPRISING REWARD

A spiritual truth that I have experienced...is that whatever we do to another we actually do to ourselves.

—Elizabeth Wessel, R.N., M.S.,
St. Joseph Health System, Orange, California

I was so struck by the above comment, posted by Ms. Wessel in the online *Journal of Sacred Work,* that I wanted to highlight it for this meditation. What if what she says is true? What if "whatever we do to another we actually do to ourselves"?

If we lived this truth and followed the winding path to compassion, imagine the impact on our lives. This nurse's observation is a concise explanation of the reason that true caregiving—those extra Samaritan-like efforts special people make—is so rewarding.

Why are we surprised when caregiving ends up blessing us in surprising ways? Perhaps because we may have, at the beginning, reached out begrudgingly. "I don't really want to make this extra effort," some part of our mind tells us. But the heart says yes. And in the giving, we receive. "I'm was so surprised by how good I felt after helping someone I didn't really want to help," I often hear caregivers say.

Equally powerful is the impact of the unkind things we do. Each time we strike a blow against another in a mean-spirited way, the near edge of the blade cuts us. When we wound another, we wound ourselves.

If we need rewards for our behavior (and most of us do), this may well be all we need to know to motivate us toward love. But we need to go beyond just the *knowing*. We must *absorb* this truth into our being so that it guides our actions.

When we hate another, we are harming ourselves. Consider the toxic feeling that wells up in you whenever you allow your energy to focus on the deeds of some enemy. And when we consciously ignore a cry for help, we also hurt ourselves. We know this is true, don't we? I think of times I've been mean or selfish and know how this has wounded me as well as the other.

We all carry the scars of our own cruelty. Yet these scars begin to heal as we reach to help another beyond our own need. When we love another, we heal ourselves as well. That is the surprising gift of loving care. The calling of caregiving is to love people who often seem "unlovable." The reward is that, when we live love, God's light illuminates our souls.

ON HOPE

Inside everyone is a great shout of energy waiting to be born.

—David Whyte

Fatigue enters the life of every committed caregiver. In those times, no matter how committed and loving, the prospect of facing one more patient or one more client or one more phone call can seem overwhelming.

If you're feeling strong at the moment you read this, it may be difficult to recall the bone-tired exhaustion you have felt at those other harder times. The emptiness at the end of working a double-shift, the way you felt at the end of child labor right before your baby was born, or simply the fatigue you feel when the alarm erupts before dawn. In the comfort of your own bed, the temptation to hide there can feel very appealing. And then some pinprick of light appears, first a bother, then recognized as the glow of hope rising from someone calling to you for help. Off in the distance, you are needed. And your humanity will rise, once again, to greet that hopeful need with your love.

What does hope look like when she interferes with our relaxation? What color and shape does she take and how do we welcome her arrival at the edge of our eyes?

Last Hope

Last eve when I merged with the dusk
and the new night began to swallow
*   the only light left in the final corner*
of my heart. Last eve, since I couldn't stop
her, I let the night darken me with her soft
*   blanket. Hope's moon was sheathed in clouds*
and I rested unseen beneath the covers.
Why not let what's left dissolve into the
*   powerful black? Darkness is for hiding and*
black can be a kind partner if you want to
turn your back on everyone's demands. No

one can command the invisible, can they?
I was tired and never wanted to work again.
The wind settled and the lightless night grew
heavy and everyone and everything was gone
except for something, out on the edge
of my right eye, an irritation, a single firefly soft-
blinking from his lighthouse a solitary yes.

—E.C.

Who among us has not tried to hide from need beneath the comfortable covers of indifference? It is human to love, and it is also human to seek our own rest. In the middle of the night, the baby cries. Who will rise and why? In the middle of the day, a call light comes on at the nurse station. It's that pesky patient again.  Who will respond? The Alzheimer's patient wants you to sit with her a little longer and you're tired and you know she won't remember whether you were there or not. She looks up at you with the tears of need in her eyes. Will you lend her hope your presence for awhile?

UNCONDITIONAL LOVE—
THE CASE OF CASEY

Why do people love their pets so much? Look at this little photo and see if you don't feel better. Meet Casey, my younger sister Martha's dog. Martha is a caregiver at The Toledo Hospital in Toledo, Ohio. Each day, she greets hundreds of visitors in her role as receptionist at the front desk. She does her job so well that last year she was named employee of the year at this large hospital.

How do you keep up your energy in such a demanding job, especially when many people are asking you the same questions every day? As she comes home tired at the end of her work, Martha knows she can count on something special from Casey—unconditional affection.

As you may know from direct experience, animals can be wonderful caregivers. Alive Hospice in Nashville engages the help of a partner who brings both cats and dogs to visit patients. Hospice at Riverside in Columbus, Ohio, used to have a marvelous dog named Libby. Libby wore a name badge on her collar and was, with due respect to the rest of the staff, the most popular caregiver in the place.

The most striking thing I recall about Libby is the stories the staff would tell about Libby's caregiving. One patient, distraught over her terminal illness, withdrew into herself so completely that she refused to speak. One night, the nurse found the patient lying on the floor hugging Libby and weeping as she spoke for the first time in a week. Throughout, Libby lay quiet.

Dogs and cats don't pass judgment. They don't mind if a patient has lost all her hair and they don't mind lying still for hours as patients on the edge of life stroke their ears or confess their heart's pain.

The Case of Casey is open and shut. He is a caregiver's caregiver. And I know he brings energy and hope to my sister every day—just as he did for you when you gazed into his warm brown eyes a few moments ago.

TOUGH-MINDED AND TENDER-HEARTED

We must always be tough-minded and tender-hearted at the same time.

—Martin Luther King Jr.

One of the most common mistakes people make in interpreting loving care is the notion that it's only about kindness and compassion. Some executives (usually my fellow males, I'm sorry to say) try to demean the work of Radical Loving Care by barking: "Oh, is this some of that touchy-feely stuff?"

This ridiculous phrase demonstrates a deep misunderstanding of the nature of love. Loving care requires a combination of discipline, competence, and courage balanced with caring and compassion. The most loving thing a physical therapist may need to do is to compel a stiff-jointed patient to move—even when that movement will cause short-term pain. A good counselor, to be effective, may need to push his client to confront his or her worst fears in order to gain healing. A leader may need to remove a supervisor that is engaging in bullying behavior.

Yet people will still say to me: How can we be loving in the middle of laying people off?

There's a simple answer to this question. Layoffs can be handled with respect, compassion, and caring. In fact, *it's during the hard times when love is needed the most*. It's easy to be loving toward nice patients. It's hard to be loving toward rude ones. It's easy to be generous when there's plenty of money in the budget. It's harder to be generous when money is tight.

Martin Luther King Jr. led a mission grounded in love. To lead this mission required that he awaken in the hearts of all Americans a sense of compassion for mistreated minorities. To carry forward his mission required the tough discipline and hard courage of asking his followers to face fire hoses, abuse, and imprisonment to accomplish loving objectives. Nonviolence became a profile of loving behavior—a classic example of turning the other check.

Touchy-feely? Hardly. Courageous men and women know that loving care is not for the faint of heart. It requires deep commitment and a profound belief in the power of our humanity to heal the pain of others.

Next time you hear anyone grumble about loving care as "touchy-feely," ask them one question: How would they like their mother to be treated if she needs hospitalization, or needs to go to a nursing home, or has been raped, or is terminally ill in a hospice? The phrase "tough-minded, tender-hearted" takes on new meaning when it is you, or your loved one that needs healing from strangers.

REFLECTION
What does it mean to you to be simultaneously tough-minded and tender-hearted in your life work? When does love require tough-minded and disciplined thinking?

COURAGEOUS CAREGIVERS

On National Public Radio (NPR) recently, a reporter interviewed doctors and nurses in a burn unit treating soldiers suffering the exhausting and exquisite agony of severe burns. One soldier had been flown in from the front lines of the Iraq War. He entered the hospital more than a year ago with burns over 97% of his body. "These patients never survive," a doctor said. "But somehow this fellow did." It took over four hundred days of radical loving care to bring about this miracle.

"In this work," a nurse said, "you either celebrate glorious success or your heart is broken."

Every doctor and nurse knows that burn patients are among the hardest challenges to treat. Treatment requires a painstaking commitment with limited chances of success. The work is more often heartbreaking than glorious. Who takes care of these courageous caregivers who, each day, face the prospect of treating these horribly wounded patients—the ones most people don't want to look at, much less treat?

The answer is that psychological support is offered, but it's often not enough. One nurse who has seen many of his patients die has a place where he stops each day to cry for the patients he has lost. Another says, "You just have to cram these losses down into some part of you and move on because there are six more people waiting for your help."

Today, if you're the praying kind, send up some of your prayers for these suffering patients. These are men and women who once posed for pictures in their dress uniforms, healthy, proud, and energetic, and now lie suffering in spite of the best efforts of their physicians.

And pray for their caregivers, those remarkably committed few who work in one of the hardest centers in any war: the burn unit. These people are among the many unsung and heroic caregivers who offer their healing presence to those whose lives are fragile and pain-filled. These are the people who, at this very moment, are finding the courage to stand close to the fires of war. They offer their love to heal the horror and hatred that has brought pain into the lives of so many.

During the Viet Nam War, Mother Teresa was asked if she would join an anti-war protest. "No," she said, "I will not march AGAINST. But if you want to march FOR *peace*, I will be glad to join you."

Today, add one more prayer to your list. Pray for peace.

PRAYER REFLECTION

> *Lord who is Love, bring your strength*
> *to the suffering. Let the river of your*
> *grace flow across the skin of the burned*
> *to cool their pain. Bring your light into*
> *the eyes of those who care for these*
> *patients. Bless them, love them, bring*
> *them the peace that comes only*
> *through you.*

SACRED EYES

Our task is to become aware of God's presence... We are called to see differently and then to live differently.

—Sallie McFague, PhD., *Life Abundant*

W hy is it that some caregivers seem to have such a genius for caregiving? Could it be that, as Dr. Sallie McFague says, they have learned to see differently and, therefore, they live differently?

The best definition of God I have ever seen is the one offered by both the apostles Paul and John. God is Love. The latest polls show that over ninety percent of Americans say they believe in God. If they were asked if they believed in love, perhaps the percentage would be even higher.

Dr. McFague says that "we are instruments of divine love" and, since "we were created in God's image, in the image of love, our goal is to grow more fully into that image by loving each other and the world in concrete ways." Those who have learned to let God's love flow through them are the ones in whom we see this genius gift of caregiving. Perhaps they have done nothing more than get out of the way so that love can flow through them.

But what about the rest of us? If we are having trouble loving, it might be because we fight love instead of surrendering to it. We fall victim to the original sin—Pride. In so doing, we pit our limited strength against love's unlimited power.

Mozart, one of the most widely acknowledged geniuses in history, claimed that he was only a scribe, writing down the music that flowed through him. "Love, love, love," he said. "That is the soul of genius." An astonishing footnote to his genius is that his music manuscripts remain almost entirely free of corrections. He simply wrote down what he heard.

It requires a great deal of courage and commitment for us to peel away all the layers of noise around us so that we can hear the voice of love and do love's biding. So many crosscurrents confuse our pathway. Our challenge, as Dr. McFague says so well, is to learn how to see differently and then to live differently. This means, in caregiving, letting go of self and replacing self with other. It means learning to see the other *and* ourselves with sacred eyes. For, as children of God, we are children of love.

Each of us needs to travel our own inner pathway toward this truth. Why? Because the voyage to God leads to love.

REVIEW AND RENEW

Take some time now and then to review your meditations of the past week. Are your reflections becoming more meaningful? Do you feel yourself learning how to find your center, to re-balance? If these things remain difficult, part of the meditative experience involves accepting the discomfort of temporary imbalance. Grief, sadness, and pain are great teachers. Yet there is no need to wallow there. Today, as you reflect on this past week's experience, take time for gratitude. Gratitude is the greatest gift and the finest way to help us recover the balance that we, as caregivers, need so that we may let love pass through us to others.

Read back through your past week's meditations. See if they raise different thoughts for you than they did when you first read them. Today, write your own meditation as a gift to yourself.

THE ROBOT CRISIS?

O wonder!
How many goodly creatures are there here!
How beauteous mankind is!
O brave new world,
That has such people in't!

—Shakespeare, *The Tempest*, Act V, Scene 1

It was from these hopeful lines of Shakespeare that writer Aldous Huxley drew the title for his terrifying novel of human degradation, *Brave New World* (1932). In the novel, the human spirit is challenged. What makes us human? Do we need humanity?

The question echoes even louder today. Continuing advances in medical and computer technology raise questions that strike at the heart of our humanity. Could a robot be created to replicate a human being in every respect?

Before you dismiss this question out of hand, consider what could be done in the foreseeable future. It is possible to envision the day when virtually every physical element of the human body might be artificially created, from our skin, bones, flesh, and eyes, down to our hearts (already possible). Copying the physical body—even without cloning—is now imaginable.

What about thinking? Robots can already be programmed to perform many aspects of our brain function. Computers already execute many analytical tasks far more effectively than humans. They can analyze, calculate, and mimic the expression of human feeling.

What is left? What about the soul? What about love? Isn't love the most distinguishing element of our humanity?

I asked a Harvard scientist, an expert in endocrinology, this question. "For me," she said, "love is something you do."

"Something you do?" I repeated. "But what about the feeling and intention that underlies loving behavior?" I asked.

"I don't know," she replied.

Her response, including her uncertainty about the role of feeling, chilled me. I know this woman well and know her to be a loving, kind, and caring human being. Does she think a robot could be manufactured that

could do just as well? Every part of my humanity rejects this proposition. Is this just human egocentrism? I hope not.

First, I believe we have souls—the spirit of God that lives within us cannot be concocted by any scientist. Second, I believe humanity is unique to our very being. Third, I believe human courage is unique. Fourth, the human capacity to love—and the thoughts that generate love—cannot be replicated.

Robots can be developed that would perform transactional tasks better than humans. This is, in fact, often a good use for robots. And they can also be programmed to mimic some of the *doing* aspects of what looks like loving behavior.

A recent news story profiled new Japanese robots that have been programmed to offer affectionate sounds in ways that are comforting to the addled elderly. Frighteningly, these pets were developed because of a decline in the commitment of younger people to visit their elders. Now, some say, why bother to visit granny if a robot can perform this task for them?

But the human spirit, and human feeling, by definition, can never appear in something mechanical. The best a robot can do is *mimic* human actions, not the *feeling* that generates them.

By definition, a robot can never establish a *human* relationship with a human. A robot can never develop the ability to love a human. A robot can never be a child of God.

For me, that's the essence of the answer. It is the basis of Radical Loving Care and the notion of the Sacred Encounter. What a human being seeks, in their darkest hours, is not programmed words of comfort from a robot, but human presence—the knowing that the individual before him or her truly cares. Human companionship is the only remaining defense against the loneliness and potential isolation of illness. That is the greatest meaning caregivers may draw from the sacred nature of their work. That only they, as compassionate people, can offer that unique human expression—love. Love is God's gift, not a creation of science.

I hope I'm right. God help us if I'm not.

REFLECTION FROM THE 13TH CENTURY

Surrender
Weep, and then smile . . .

—Jalaluddin Rumi (1207–1273)

Over the last seven centuries, millions of people of all faiths have, on occasion, turned to the wisdom and beauty of the great 13th-century Persian poet known as Rumi. Like so many in the world, Rumi reportedly grew up in a difficult childhood environment. Yet he grew to become one of the great masters of Sufi thought and practice and a sage for the ages.

Rumi's message speaks to all those who seek to love others in the best spirit of our humanity. His belief was that when we open our hearts to others, we are opening our hearts to God. He preached surrender to God's love.

Let some of his words, passed on to me by a reader of the online *Journal of Sacred Work*, speak to you and move through you as you contemplate your work as a caregiver over the past week, your plans for the week to come, and your celebration of your now—your time of rest.

> *Surrender*
> *Weep, and then smile.*
> *Don't pretend to know something*
> *you haven't experienced.*
>
> *There's a necessary dying,*
> *and then Jesus is breathing again.*
>
> *Very little grows*
> *on jagged rock.*
> *Be ground.*
>
> *Be crumbled,*
> *so wildflowers will come up*
> *where you are.*

You've been stony for too many years.
Try something different.
Surrender.

—Rumi

REFLECTION

How hard it is to accept the message of surrender to God—of surrender to love. Depending upon how we were raised, we may have felt the lifelong message that our job is to assert our will, to be strong and NOT to surrender. Now we hear the message of faith—surrender to God's love and live in God's grace.

LEARNING TO BE A CAREGIVER—A STORY

It's the sense of touch . . . In any real city, you walk past other people, brush against them. In L.A. nobody touches you, we're always behind this metal and glass. I think we miss that touch so much that we crash into each other just so we can feel something.

—opening lines from the movie "Crash"

Jean was tired. On the job for only three weeks, she wondered if nursing was really for her. "I thought the nurse's aides would handle bedpans," she moaned to her charge nurse as she washed her hands. "I didn't go to nursing school for this."

Lorraine the charge nurse lifted her coffee mug off the counter and invited Jean to sit down. "Why *did* you go to nursing school? It can't have been because you wanted to get rich…"

"I'm a nurse because I want to help cure sick people. But yesterday, I spent twenty minutes shaving that stroke patient, Mr. Johansson. We could call a barber to do stuff like that."

"How did Mr. Johansson seem after you shaved him?"

"Because of his stroke, he didn't say much. But he smiled a little."

"How do you think he felt after you cleaned off his face?" Lorraine asked.

"Better, I suppose."

"So you made him feel better without giving him any medication or doing any other procedures on him? And he knows you're a nurse who's doing something extra to help him?"

"Yes. But he's still paralyzed," Jean said.

"That's right. Can you cure his paralysis?"

"No."

"What *can* you do then? What does he need from you?"

"I don't know," Jean said. "To me, his situation is hopeless. All I can feel for him is pity. He's an old man and his life is over. He'll probably never walk again. It's just pathetic."

"That's giving him pity," Lorraine said. "What does he really need from you?"

"I can do the basic stuff for him—put in IVs, make sure his monitors are working, feed him…"

"That's what his *body* needs. What else does *he* need?"

"If you're talking about spiritual stuff, I can call the chaplain for that," Jean grumbled.

"Yes," Lorraine replied, "we can call the chaplain. But what can *you* give him?"

Jean sat and thought. After a few moments, her eyes brightened, "Maybe I could give him hope?" Then her face darkened. "But the truth is, he's not going to recover."

"How do you give hope to a patient who won't recover?" Lorraine asked. "What would you do for this man if he *were* your father?"

"I would love him—kiss his cheek, hold his hand, tell him I care about him, sit by his side, read to him. But he's not my father."

"He's someone's father, or brother, or husband, isn't he?" Lorraine said. "And if he has no family, then he needs you even more. Can you love him in ways you learned to love others you love?"

"I can try," Jean said.

"And when you do all these things—take care of his body and also love him as a person," Lorraine said, "you will have given his humanity *your* humanity. Only then will you be a true nurse."

THE MAGIC OF AWARENESS

What is necessary to change a person is to change his awareness of himself.

—Abraham Maslow (1908–1970)

H ere it is, the formula for our transformation in one sentence. Maslow's statement may be true, but this level of actualization is hardly as simple as his words suggest. In fact, Maslow placed it toward the top of his hierarchy of human needs—the last layer before transcendence. How do we change our awareness of ourselves for the better?

This process is critical for caregivers because, by definition, caregivers are engaged in helping *other* people through times of great change. If I come to you in need of loving care and your self-image is that you are not a very loving person, we've both got a problem.

One of the core truths in our teaching at the Healing Trust is that, *Where attention goes, energy flows.* I have repeated this statement to audiences and to myself thousands of times. Each time, the truth of it ripples through me with renewed power. I know I need to periodically check my attention because it is so easy for it to turn negative, stirring poison within. As Maslow suggests, if I'm feeling negative energy, it's time for me to change myself by becoming aware of my thoughts and the circling of my energy.

The best, short-term way to reverse negative thinking is *not* to tell yourself to quit thinking a certain thought but to replace negative thinking with positive thinking—to replace negative images with positive ones. If I try *not* to think a negative thought, this means I must first think of it again. If I *replace* the negative thought with a positive one, the negative image fades back, even though it may not disappear. It requires a new awareness, a new set of what Peter Senge called "mental models" for us to change long-ingrained awareness patterns.

So, longer term, what is my basic awareness of myself? If I think of myself as generally discouraged, how do I change that? One way, of course, is to consciously turn my energy toward something positive.

As a simple example, on the way to work yesterday morning, I caught myself in a negative thought pattern about a person in my life I find trou-

blesome. I realized my body was tensing as if headed into battle when in fact I see this person rarely and knew I would not even see him that day. Why am I allowing this person to dominate my moods and cause my tension to rise?

I needed to be *aware* of what was happening and identify it as a negative thought pattern. Next, I needed to change my awareness—either to think of this person in a new way (the best choice) or to consciously think of something else.

In that particular case, I took an easy way out. I simply turned on some of my favorite classical music and let my attention move to the flow of the notes. My anxiety began to ease immediately and soon my awareness was positive and productive. In addition, I regained perspective. There was no need to let another person control the balance and agenda of my day.

It's not always that easy. But practicing this approach in simple situations may help us when we deal with more complex problems.

Practice. Meditate. Become aware of yourself as touched by a Divine Spark. As a carrier of love, you carry beauty within you! Integrate this image into a new self-image. With practice, your sense of love will increasingly shine through your eyes and through all aspects of life. You will be more aligned with God.

Enough

Enough. These few words are enough.
If not these words, this breath.
If not this breath, this sitting here.
This opening to the life
we have refused
again and again
until now.
Until now.

—David Whyte

ON SELF-KINDNESS AND EMPATHY

To empathize, you recall within yourself a time when you felt even a particle or thread of what another person now seems to feel. With that beginning, you continue to listen carefully with your heart...coming as close as you can to appreciating what his or her experience is like. You don't try to duplicate it within you—you just stay with it, fathoming it as well as you can.

—from *The Art of Being a Healing Presence*,
James E. Miller with Susan C. Cutshall

A colleague and friend of mine has a ten-year-old daughter. Recently, she came to him and said, "Daddy, I think I'm too dumb and too fat."

What does a father say? It requires empathy to know how to respond to heart-breaking comments like this. But how does a man in his forties empathize with the feelings of a ten-year old girl? What we know is true is that the more he can empathize, the more likely he is to come up with a good answer.

An *unthinking* answer goes like this: "Stop feeling that way. You're not dumb and you're not fat." This answer denies the person's feelings and doesn't help resolve them.

Equally foolish is the comment blurted out by so many people when someone shares their personal pain: "I know *exactly* how you feel!" None of us knows exactly how another person feels and to say so is unempathetic and denies the uniqueness of the pain the other is experiencing. As Miller and Cutshall say, we don't have to try to duplicate someone else's feelings in order to be empathetic.

So how do we become present to another?

Haven't all of us felt dumb or the wrong weight or experienced some other feeling of self-doubt at some time in our lives? Certainly, my friend has. And that's the feeling he had to get in touch with in order to help.

What we all want in situations like that is to have people empathize with how hard it is to feel inadequate. Of course, my friend's daughter isn't dumb and, at ten, she does not have a weight problem. But what if she did? The solution won't come from stern parental warnings. It will more likely

flow from kindness and empathy. Here's roughly what my friend said to his daughter:

Dad: Do you believe in being kind to other people?

Daughter: Yes. Of course.

Dad: Then what about being kind to yourself?

Accusing ourselves of deficiencies doesn't solve them. Worse, self-cruelty may make it harder for us to empathize with others. If we judge ourselves harshly, we are more likely to pass harsh judgment on others. What if I had a weight problem and I beat myself up about it emotionally? I go on a diet. Now, how do I look at someone else with an apparent weight problem? Suddenly, I may find myself passing judgment on them just as I did on myself. After all, I've lost weight, why haven't they?

Assume, on the other hand, that what I really have is a self-esteem problem and, accordingly, I eat more food to try to fill my emotional void. Of course, the food generates only a temporary feeling of comfort, perhaps fooling me into thinking that the more food I eat, the less inadequate I will feel.

If I can learn to be kinder in my self-talk, however, there is a greater chance my self-esteem will improve. My eating problem may then begin to resolve through the practice of self-kindness.

This is the theory and it's not hard to understand. Clearly, reversing a lifetime of negative self-talk is far more difficult. Caregivers need to prioritize this personal change because kindness to self enables us to better give our hearts to others during their need—and to help them practice self-kindness.

Reach out with empathy to someone today. There is someone you will (or can choose to) encounter today who would love to have your understanding and your kindness. Take the opportunity to practice empathy with them. Listen with your eyes rather then judge with your mind. You don't need to say you know how they feel, all you need to say are things like, "that must be so hard." Mostly, though, you can offer the warmth of your presence.

And remember the words of a father to his daughter. If you believe in being kind to others, start with yourself!

REFLECTIVE PRACTICE

- During your meditation, reflect on some of the kind things you've done for others.

- Remember that you are a child of God, touched by the Divine Spark. This is not an egocentric thing to say or think, it is a lovely truth that carries a beautiful responsibility with it to let love flow through you.

Again: Remember to reach out with empathy to someone today. Take the opportunity to practice empathy with them. Listen rather then judge. Unwrap for them your gift of love.

JOY

*Inside everyone
is a great shout of joy
waiting to be born.*

—David Whyte, *The House of Belonging*

Among the many things hanging in my office is a handmade sign with one word on it: Yes.

"Why the sign?" lots of people ask me.

"Because I need to remember," I usually respond.

In a world filled with conflict, grief, hostility, and frustration, it is easy to forget the yes of life—to forget that "inside everyone is a great shout of joy waiting to be born." When do we give birth to our joy and how do we do that?

Part of the difficulty in releasing our shout of joy flows from the way many of us confuse joy with happiness. Happiness is a bouncing ball which drops into our lives with a perplexing randomness. My two-year-old grandson can shift from sad to happy (or vice versa) in a split second based on the skill of his parents in shifting his attention or his own idea of whether he likes what's in front of him or not. His happy/sad dance looks simple. Ours may feel more nuanced and complex. Yet both seem to rest on shifting sands.

Joy, once understood and developed, rests on steadier ground. Joy flows from faith in God or belief in love. To me, they're the same thing.

Joy is an energy that, once released, graces our lives to the end of our days.

Grief lives in us as well. We grieve our fundamental loneliness and we grieve the periodic loss of those who seemed to free us from the pain of isolation's trap.

David Whyte's poetic wisdom speaks to us again: "I have my few griefs and joys/I can call my own/and through accident it seems,/ a steadfast faith in each of them/and that's what I will say/ matters when the story ends."

For many caregivers, Joy struggles for air beneath an ocean of grief connected to the pain they work with each day or night (or both). It's time to free this Joy so that it may balance and inform our grief rather than be drowned by it. When Joy is freed from within, grief becomes tolerable as

her subordinate. We can live through grief's storms because of the sure knowledge that the sun lives above the black roof of clouds.

Today is the day for us to shout our Yes to the world, to let her rich voice sing through the rest of our days and nights.

REFLECTIVE PRACTICE

The journey to freeing Joy begins with the practice of gratitude. Reflect today on the many gifts of your life. Start with the remembrance that you are a child of God's love.

To read and hear more of David Whyte's work, go to www.davidwhyte.com

DIALOGUE WITH THE SACRED

Every sacred place is a place where eternity shines through time.

—Joseph Campbell

With loving care, a Japanese garden was created several years back as a sacred space on the outskirts of Nashville. It offers its peaceful presence in the middle of a searingly beautiful park called Cheekwood.

The first time I visited the garden, I paused to read a small sign that recommended traveling the garden path slowly in order to appreciate the many fine details of nature and occasional small sculptures that live along the way. Partway through my journey, I entered a thick stand of bamboo. The stalks swayed in the breeze, tapping each other in rhythmic conversation. Amid the beauty and grace of the garden, something strange happened.

A family of four, including two children in their early teens, came charging through as if escaping a house fire. One of the teens was running. "Come on," the father said to the other teen, "there's more stuff to see over by the lake."

On the heels of the family of four was a woman in her twenties talking on a cell phone. "So what did Bobby *say?*" she shouted into the phone as she walked by me, staring at the ground.

I don't know what Bobby said, but it took some effort for me to ease back into the experience of listening to the voice of the garden, what she had to say to me or to anyone who slowed long enough to listen to her songs. Perhaps, more than anything, what she did was help me to hear my own music.

Yes, it can sound judgmental to criticize others for seeming to ignore the sacred experiences before their eyes. Yet we are all surrounded by noise and distractions and we often create them ourselves.

A place may be sacred, but for a sacred *experience* to occur, a dialogue must be opened between the place and the person. And there must be a genuine pause, a silence that allows the sacred to speak to us. Otherwise, the sacred is nothing more than a piece of ground or a pile of stones.

www.journalofsacredwork.typepad.com

A Christian may enter a mosque, a Muslim may enter Notre Dame, a Jew may enter a Buddhist shrine, or a Hindu a synagogue, and gather nothing of the sacred that lives there for others. A tourist may stand before the ancient shapes of Stonehenge or the mysterious smile of the Mona Lisa and feel nothing. Each of these encounters will lack the resonance needed for the sacred to shine through *unless* each person approaches the sacred place of others with special respect and an openness to the universality of God's beauty.

An openness and a dialogue is required in order for a vibration with the sacred to occur.

So long as any caregiver sees the homeless as lazy, bad, and troublesome, no love will flow through the encounter. So long as caregivers think of patients as gall bladders or hips or kidneys, instead of whole human beings, the sacred will be blocked off. So long as caregivers scorn patient gowns as signs of lowliness and weakness instead of robes deserving respect, the people wearing them will never receive the healing care they need.

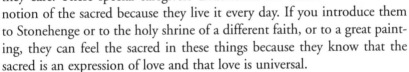

Fortunately, there are many caregivers across this land who appreciate the gift that caregiving offers. For them, each shift they work is an opportunity to open a sacred dialogue between their hearts and the pain of those for whom they care. These special caregivers understand the whole notion of the sacred because they live it every day. If you introduce them to Stonehenge or to the holy shrine of a different faith, or to a great painting, they can feel the sacred in these things because they know that the sacred is an expression of love and that love is universal.

How does eternity shine through time? It happens millions of times a day, when caregivers open their hearts and let God's love travel through them and into the heart of a person in need. And they feel something else, as the love they give travels back through them and back to them in a sacred circle. Because of this truth, any fluorescent-lit corner of linoleum in a hospital or hospice or other charity can instantly become sacred. Because any place love finds expression becomes a place where eternity shines through time.

WHO TAUGHT YOU LOVE?

As you continue to send out love, the energy returns to you in a regenerating spiral... As love accumulates, it keeps your system in balance and harmony.

—Sara Paddison

From whom did you learn love? Your mother, your grandmother, your father, a friend, a complete stranger, your own child, a group?

I first learned love from the woman in this photograph. She turned ninety-four on August 21, 2006. Along with my three siblings, I am unusually fortunate to have my mother still here on this earth at such an

advanced age. Her early mother's gifts enabled me to receive love from other, later, givers. And, hopefully, to learn to give love myself.

We can all say about our mothers that without them we wouldn't exist. But that is, in part, a comment on biology that covers fathers as well. Most people experience love in the very

first moments of their lives from the person who carried them within their own bodies for nine months or so. Our mother's love comes to us as she holds us against her in our first moments. But our mothers are not always the turning-point people in our lives.

Some are unlucky. They may lose their mothers at birth or are born through women who find it difficult to love. So where else can we learn love?

Who taught you to offer kindness beyond your own needs? Since caregivers are the ones who love those in need, today is a day to contemplate those who have taught love by giving it to *you*.

During a gathering of former prostitutes at a retreat for an organization called Magdalene, I learned something new about love. In a circle sat about twenty-five women, most of them former prostitutes and drug addicts tracking the path to recovery. I asked each of them, "From whom did you learn love?" Several women shed tears as they recalled grandpar-

ents, parents, aunts and uncles, and whole neighborhoods that had taught them love.

Toward the end, one woman, a recovering prostitute and former drug addict in her early thirties, gave an answer I'll never forget. "No one ever taught me love," she said. "For me, love was something I sold on the street for $60 an hour. Then I came to Magdalene." She paused, looked around the room. "The first time I ever saw love was from these people," she said. "They did things for me and never asked anything in return. They were kind to me even when I wasn't kind to them. I never felt love until I entered this community."

Communities can teach love. And they can also reinforce it. Magdalene teaches love not by offering a course, but by living it and by giving it.

If you have been lucky enough to receive love in your life and wise enough to live love every day, then this is a time to recall your teachers— the lovely men and women and children who helped you know that you were, and are, loved.

Imagine the people for whom *you* have been the one who taught them love. And think of all those who may yet receive the gifts of your heart.

You are a child of love. And a caring mother's love remains among the most beautiful early examples of kindness as she gives herself to a helpless one in need—the contact with her skin, the soothing tones of her voice, her warm embrace.

Love that comes later can be complex and hard to come by. Yet we long for it at our most vulnerable moments. Perhaps this is why hardened soldiers, wounded in the middle of battle, call first for their mothers.

Celebrate, today, your teachers of love. And be a teacher for others— not through instruction, but through example. Give away the most precious gift you have—and feel it circle back through you.

THE EVEREST OF THE HEART

A British mountaineer, desperate for oxygen, had collapsed on a well-traveled route to the [Everest] summit. Dozens of people walked right past him, unwilling to risk their own ascents. Within hours, David Sharp, 34, was dead.

—AP 5/27/06

Ever since Mount Everest was identified as the world's tallest peak in 1852 (and named Everest in 1856), people have sought to climb its peak. Mount Everest became a sort of Holy Grail for some as they sought to test the limits of their skill and strength by climbing her. A century of efforts passed before Sir Edmund Hillary and his Sherpa guide, Tenzeng Norgay, finally ascended the peak on May 29, 1953. They were hailed worldwide as heroes. Since then, hundreds more have tried and succeeded and many more have failed.

Ascending Everest is still an accomplishment that requires skill, endurance, planning, persistence, and a stout heart. Apparently, though, it does not require the presence of a compassionate heart. The opportunity to compare the above story to that of the Good Samaritan is tempting. Dozens of people saw a fellow human in need and, like the priest and the Levite in the parable, "walked right past him."

How often do we ignore the needs of others in favor of our own goals? How do we, as caregivers, find the balance necessary to give love and accomplish personal success at the same time?

The short answer is that we always succeed whenever we give love. Presence to the needs of another is the highest expression of the self.

Many, including Sir Edmund himself, were outraged that, on the morning of May 15, 2006, no one stopped to help the stricken David Sharp (who had already ascended the summit and was on his way down when he fell ill.) In fact, one group did stop briefly and offer Mr. Sharp oxygen, but then chose to go on their way, leaving him to die.

It's easy for us, sitting comfortably somewhere near sea level, to pass judgment on those battling wind, cold, and low oxygen at an altitude of 29,000 feet. Still, it is clear that a number of climbers chose their own goals and ignored love's calling to help a weakened brother.

Amazingly, on May 26, only days later, another climber, Australian Lincoln Hall became stranded in the same fashion as David Sharp. Again, many climbers passed by. But this time, a group led by climber Dan Mazur stopped to help. Surrendering their own goals to reach the summit (they were within two hours of the peak), Mr. Mazur's group (including two clients who had paid him to help them reach the summit) dedicated their lives and their supplies to saving the life of Mr. Hall. In true Samaritan style, they did not give up until Mr. Hall had been both saved and given followup care.

In failing to reach the peak, Mazur's group climbed an "Everest" far more important. They saved a human life by giving of themselves. They abandoned personal goals and took up the goal of helping another.

"I don't know why [others] didn't stop to help," Mazur said. And he added that if he was ever in that state, he hoped a passerby would be "someone like me."

Mazur lived the Golden Rule. Here is what this story can tell us: *Climbing the Everest of the Heart is harder than climbing the Everest of the Himalayas.*

Mountain climbing requires a personal commitment to skill, training, brains and brawn. Living love requires a depth of courage and love far greater than any of these. To live love, we must climb a peak that requires the courage to face our darkest corners and to surrender our will to the call of love. We must scale the heavens and open our hearts to that love that lives on the other side of our own personal need. It is a climb that calls to us each day. We can ignore it and, like many, pass it by. Or we can stop and embrace it.

What does a Samaritan look like? Dan Mazur looks ordinary enough on the outside. Like all of us his soul is invisible. Does he have the skill to scale Everest? His resumé shows that he does. Did love flow through him on the morning of May 26? Clearly, it did. Just ask the man whose life he saved.

Each of us faces opportunities, large and small, to climb the Everest of our hearts. Today, a caregiver will want to pass by the voice calling in need from a patient room. After all, as many caregivers have told me, there are always people calling out for help from their rooms or from stretchers or on the street or from images of places like sub-Saharan Africa, or Haiti, or New Orleans.

In some cases, the call comes from far away and we can comfort ourselves that far away is *too* far for us. But many calls will come to us from people well within our reach. We will often have the choice to *interrupt* our journey toward our own goals. We can choose to stop, offer a friendly touch, the soft eyes of our compassion and the full help another may need from us, or we can walk on by. It can be a hard mountain to climb, yet at its peak is the only summit worth reaching.

REFLECTIVE PRACTICE

■ After Hillary and Norgay climbed Everest, Hillary said, "We didn't know if it was humanly possible to climb Everest." Indeed, in a hundred years since its discovery, no one had done so. If you had been Hillary, would you have stopped to help another stranded climber if you had encountered one—and possibly given up your chance for immortality?

■ When we don't stop to help, there are always excuses and explanations, but what does our failure to stop say about our values?

■ Is it fair for us to pass judgment on those who don't stop or, for that matter, to praise those who do?

■ Do you agree that we don't always need to travel to a faraway place to find adventure and opportunity to serve? Is the Everest of the heart truly harder to climb than the actual mountain?

■ What have you done to reach out to help another beyond your own need?

■ What is the most important thing you will do (or have done) to help someone today?

THE CALL OF OUR TRUE NATURE

. . . Ask me whether what I have done is my life . . .
You and I can turn and look at the silent river and wait.
We know the current is there, hidden; and there are
comings and goings from miles away that hold the stillness
exactly before us. What the river says, that is what I say.

—William Stafford, *Ask Me*

At five, I wanted to be a cowboy. At fifteen, I wanted to be President and give speeches like Winston Churchill. At twenty-five, I was a trial lawyer and wanted to be like Martin Luther King. At thirty-five, I was president of a hospital and wanted to be an artist. At forty-five, I was president of an Ohio hospital system and wanted to be a national television star. At fifty-five, I was president of a Tennessee hospital system and wanted to be a minister.

Ask me whether what I have done is my life. It's a challenging question. How would *you* answer it?

Parker Palmer offers us a way to find our answers in his beautiful book *Let Your Life Speak* (Jossey-Bass, 2000). The title comes from an old Quaker saying, and Palmer finds the statement profound.

Across America today, caregivers will let their lives speak either through meeting the needs of others *or* through holding back their gifts and doing the minimum. Holding back may mean they are in a career that is distant from their true nature.

We try on the costumes of different roles across our childhood and start making some decisions as adults. How can we discern if our choices are true to our nature or whether we are acting a role someone else assigned to us? "Vocation does not mean a goal I pursue," Palmer says, "but a calling I hear." He quotes twenty-one words from May Sarton:

Now I become myself
It's taken time, many years and places.
I have been dissolved and shaken,
Worn other people's faces.

Why is it so difficult to hear our true nature? We ask children and teenagers (and were once asked ourselves): What are you going to do? What are you going to be? And in these questions, we hear the expectations of others. A boy says he wants to be a dancer and may sense the disapproval of his father. A girl says she wants to become a doctor and may feel the doubts of her mother or her teachers.

Frightened by disapproval, fearful of rejection, uncertain of our gifts, we may surrender our true nature and adopt the choices others foist upon us. Mid-career, we may find ourselves wondering if our vocation is truly our calling. This answer can only be found by peeling away others' expectations to rediscover our nature.

There is a further challenge. Imbued with a sense of society's loftier values, we may feel ourselves asking what we *ought* to do rather than who we are. There is, as well, the perplexing problem of our particular potential. I may desire the career of a major league baseball player. Yet at some point I must face the truth of my skill level. If I feel called to the major leagues and am blocked by lack of talent or injury or other bad luck, how do I honor my nature?

Several years back, I was fascinated to watch Michael Jordan, the greatest basketball player in history, try his hand at baseball. Relatively speaking, he wasn't very good and was quickly demoted to the Birmingham Barons of the minor leagues. A legendary basketball player, Jordan was only a relatively ordinary baseball player. Clearly, he was best at basketball, and he abandoned the diamond to return to the court. But was baseball his nature or basketball? What about accounting, school teaching, business leadership?

Ultimately, the question may not be what job we choose, but whether we are able to express our truest and best selves across each day, whatever our job. Palmer, in quoting Frederick Buechner, offers us the best wisdom I've ever read on this subject: "Vocation [is] the place where your deep glad-ness meets the world's deep need."

This is the great gift of caregiving. Today, *if caregiving is your nature, you can be present to your own gladness as you meet the needs of others.* This does-

n't mean it's easy, but it does suggest that joy will be present to you if you are pursuing your calling.

Already , at the age of two, my grandson is beginning to try out careers. At the moment, he's not sure yet whether he wants to be a pirate or a baseball player. I guess if he chose Pittsburgh, he could be both. But as a native Bostonian, he'll likely always be a fan of the Red Sox. (I haven't suggested he be a cowboy yet.)

Whatever his ultimate choice, I hope he will let his life speak by being present to his truest nature. I hope you will do the same, letting your deepest gladness meet some part of the world's need today and every day.

Reflective Practice and Subject for Circle Group Presence

- Do you think of your work as primarily a calling or mostly a job? What is the difference?

- How is your best nature expressed in your work?

- Do you experience a sense of inner joy as you go about your work?

- Are you expressing your best gifts in your work or do you find yourself holding back?

- What would it take to express more of your nature in your work?

OUR ENERGY AGE

Recently a woman in her twenties was part of a team making a presentation to our Healing Trust for a grant. She mentioned that her charity was holding a 5K race as a fundraiser. "I'd love to enter," I said, "but you'd have to add a category for people over ninety." Instead of laughing, as I thought she would, she gave me a confused look and said, "Well, I suppose we could do that...wait, so you're ninety?"

Ouch! What does ninety look like?

Putting aside my ego damage, the truth is that to people in their twenties, most people over forty or fifty seem generically "old." So I thought of another way to think about age. The new question I have for you today is: What is your energy age? Not what the calendar says, but how you feel! And here's an even bigger question: How are you *using* the energy you have?

The answer to the first question may depend on whether you're sitting still or moving around. Or your answer may depend on the time of day you ask yourself. You may feel twenty at 9 a.m. and ninety by 10 p.m.

Who cares about age anyway, especially caregivers? Movie stars might worry about it as an element of their career success. But if you work in a hospital, hospice, or nursing care facility, you may have already gained the wisdom that we are lucky to be alive and at least healthy enough to read this book.

Most "well" adults think of themselves as younger than the calendar says. This may be partly because anyone over forty comes face to face with the image they held of forty-year-olds when *they* were twenty. It's surprising how *well* most people feel in their older years.

So instead of letting ourselves be controlled by the calendar, what if we thought of ourselves by our energy age instead of our chronological age? This kind of thinking will become more relevant with each passing year.

I would say that most of the time (especially when I don't look in the mirror or when I stand up too quickly after doing pushups) I feel about thirty. How about you?

If we can shake the trap of the calendar, look at the spiritual mirror instead of a physical one, we may find good news. The soul doesn't necessarily age, does it? We may, however, grow more open to our soul's *wisdom* and less dependent on the news about our bodies.

The real question of life is not how long we live. How are we using our life's energy while we have it? Mozart and Martin Luther King both died in their thirties, yet the music of one and the message of the other are as alive today as they were when these men left their bodies. Jesus was crucified while in his early thirties. For Christians, he is as alive to them today as he was two thousand years ago.

Spending too much of our time trying to look younger than we are may steal away time and resources we could have spent engaged in meaningful service to others. Mother Teresa and Mahatma Gandhi paid no attention to their appearance and live in our hearts as ageless. Albert Einstein and Albert Schweitzer lived a long time. However, their contributions were not dependent on the length of their lives, but on the way they used their energy and potential when they had it.

This is true of all the best caregivers. They may not be famous, but their beautiful and anonymous contributions have made the difference in the quality of life of everyone they touched.

Our souls are the part of us that came from eternity and are still in touch with it. Eternity, by definition, has no age. So the truth is that the more we let love's energy move through us, the more we are in touch with ageless light.

The idea of Energy Age may seem less concrete than the calendar, especially if we are heavily dependent on the information our senses bring. But as parts of us begin to wear out, as our eyesight dims and our hearing weakens, we may take joy in two things: 1) our energy is stronger than the calendar, and 2) our souls are ageless.

Wherever you are in your life's journey, celebrate, today, the life you have right now. You're older now than you were ten minutes ago, and you're younger than you will be ten minutes from now. But our *now* is all we have.

OUR GREAT STRENGTH

We are so much stronger than we think.

—Norman Cousins

I heard Norman Cousins speak at a conference in Denver about fifteen years ago. Most of us don't remember much about a given speaker's presentation. But I was struck by the above line, the last one Cousins delivered in a magnificent speech.

In his book *Anatomy of an Illness,* Cousins, a gifted writer and former editor of the *Saturday Evening Post*, describes his own remarkable journey from the brink of a terminal illness back to health. Diagnosed with a dreaded disease, he *laughed* his way back to health and homeostasis. That's what he claims, and the evidence of his doctors proves he's right. Given a death sentence, Cousins said Yes to life and No to his illness.

Lying deeply ill in his hospital bed, Cousins asked that films of his favorite comedians be brought to him for viewing. His favorites were the Marx brothers comedies. His caregivers say that Cousins laughed his brains out day after day. Miraculously, the symptoms of his terrible connective tissue disease gradually receded.

None of his doctors believed it. But Cousins didn't seem that surprised by his recovery when he spoke to our group back in the late '80s. He told us he knew he could beat the illness—with laughter and with hope.

We spend lots of time dwelling on our weaknesses. But human strength is often stunning. Every so often, we get a literal illustration. At least once a year, the news will carry a story about some young mother who has lifted a full-sized car off her infant child that has fallen under it. How could this be? Small women can't lift cars weighing a ton and a half. Yet it has happened time and again.

Needless to say, after the emergency has passed, the woman has no more ability to lift the car than you or I. Where did her superhuman strength come from?

Practitioners of the martial arts love to demonstrate the human capacity to break bricks with our heads or smash thick boards with our hands. Indian yogis can demonstrate to us the ability of a human being to lie on a bed of nails or to slow a heart rate down to twenty beats a minute. All of

these acts turn out to be not so much tricks as an ability to concentrate energy in a particular direction.

What is the value of this for caregivers? We have capacities to heal far beyond what we imagine. We can bring to the bedside of the sick and vulnerable the greatest power of all. Healing occurs when caregivers can mediate between human pain and the power of God's love. This is not mumbo jumbo. It is holy truth. Any caregiver with any lengthy experience can tell you of patients who have recovered against the odds.

How do these things happen? As Cousins said, "We're all so much stronger than we think."

VELOCITY

Yes, we slow pokes can see a lot.

—Thomas L. Turtle in *Scotty the Snail,* by Erie Chapman

I asked my wife what I should write today. She said, "Write about how everyone is rushing so much. People are in more of a hurry now than they were when I was a little girl. Everybody rushes around the grocery story like it's on fire. What's the big emergency?"

I don't know if people are rushing more or not, but if they are, why? We've got all these labor-saving devices—all those things that were supposed to give us more leisure time. Dishes can be dropped into machines that wash *and* dry them. Same with clothes. Food can be microwaved hot in seconds, teeth brushed electronically, cars washed in less than a minute, letters e-mailed in milliseconds.

Now that these tasks are done for us by machines, what are we doing with our free time? Are we conversing with each other at ever deeper and more sophisticated levels? Are we plumbing the depths of wisdom literature, reading more, taking greater opportunities to help our fellow humans in need?

Oops. Probably not. Most people tell me they don't *have* any free time for great endeavors. They're always in a *rush*. These same people somehow manage to keep up with the *Desperate Housewives,* track the latest *American Idol,* learn who survived on *Survivor.* Then there are videogames. Got to save time for those. And there is the computer. Computers can suck more time from our lives than anything I've encountered. Time may be cheap, it seems, but it sure ain't free.

In the years after World War II, the western world got to celebrate all the freedoms won. The victory of democracy left us to pursue our most lofty dreams. But the voice of comfort is deeply seductive. Most people used far more energy fighting the war than they did celebrating the peace. All those men and women who died for us have left us with endless choices on what to do with our time.

Some of us seem so exhausted by our choices that we squander our freedoms. Caught in the grip of velocity, we race through life as if, to quote reader Sonya Jones, our "hair is on fire." We ignore Viktor Frankl's advice that "success, like happiness, cannot be pursued; it must ensue."

Caregivers seem as harried as any group I know. Doctors rush to see the next patient, nurses rush to cover the challenges of patient demands and piles of chart work, social workers struggle with waiting lists.

Patients, on the other hand, seem to be the one group that would like to be in a hurry but isn't. Stuck in the waiting rooms of the world, patients leaf through magazines wondering when, if ever, their names will be called. One would think patients would be grateful for a chance to rest. Instead, we sit like prisoners waiting to be sentenced.

British writer and poet David Whyte speaks eloquently about the American problem with velocity. He wonders why we, like Europeans, don't all slow down. We will reach our goal if we recognize that the journey *is* the goal, he says. In his book *Crossing the Unknown Sea: Work as a Pilgrimage of Identity*, Whyte points out, "The great tragedy of speed as an answer to the complexities...of existence is that very soon we cannot recognize anything or anyone who is not traveling at the same velocity as we are."

Someone slows down, and we wonder what's wrong with them. Of course, most artists have learned to slow down to see and hear. We need to do the same and learn how to be present to what they have discovered for us.

Since we spend so much of our lives going to or coming from places, why not use these times to truly live our lives? Since the only thing we really have is our time, why not engage every moment of it now instead of looking past it to the future?

A friend of mine, a nurse named Holly, says she likes to pray at stoplights. What a fine alternative to tapping the steering wheel trying to make red turn green. Another friend uses the drive to and from work as private time to reflect on his life and loves. He doesn't turn on the radio. "Why let a voice on the radio dominate my thoughts?" he asks. "This is my time to rest and to breathe." A third friend reports that when he's stuck in a traffic jam, he likes to look around at the other drivers and think, "Great! This slowdown will give me more time to reflect."

I've never liked the old adage "haste makes waste." I don't like truths that rhyme anyway because they seem to replace real thinking with platitudes. But the waste created by haste is often life itself. In the course of racing around the grocery store, our blood pressure rises and our quality of life goes down. In the course of waiting for the next thing to happen in a good movie, we may miss the artistic experience. We may even speed through a great book just to see how it ends and, in the course of that race, lose the truth and beauty of great literature.

I like the wisdom of the author of *Flow,* Mihaly Csikszentmihalyi: "To live means to experience—through doing, feeling, thinking. Experience takes place in time, so *time is the ultimate scarce resource* we have." [emphasis added]

In a children's book I wrote called *Scotty the Snail,* Thomas L. Turtle asks his slow-moving friend Scotty this question: "Have you ever noticed all the things you and I see that the other animals don't?"

Have you noticed? Take time, now, to draw in a deep breath. Slow your breathing. Look up from your book. What you see, at a slower pace, is all the things your faster-moving friends are missing. What you see, now, is your life.

THE FRAGRANCE OF FORGIVENESS

Forgiveness is the fragrance the violet sheds on the heel that crushed it.

—Mark Twain

Thousands of marvelous quotations are attributed to Mark Twain. I think the one above is among his finest. The violet will shed her aroma on the one who crushes her to death. She does this involuntarily because she must. Her beauty requires it.

For us to spread the aroma of our forgiveness on our enemies, we must make a hard and conscious choice.

One of the hardest blows to the human condition is betrayal. We have all experienced broken trust. A dear friend of mine is dealing with this now as his wife of sixteen years leaves their home for another man. Their children watch their mother turn her back on them and wonder what they have done to provoke such an attack on their family. What is the role of forgiveness?

Betrayals occur with such frequency that they are the stuff of daily soap operas. But the real-life experience is deeply painful. And there are harder blows than an errant spouse. Recently, I heard the story of a mother whose innocent son was mistakenly shot in a drive-by shooting. What is she to think about the killer?

In spite of the Christian teaching on forgiving our enemies, the vast majority of people would respond to a tragedy like this not with love but with hatred. Revenge hangs heavy on the human condition. It requires enormous courage and deep grace to forgive—to break the bonds of this chain. The mother of the slain son went far beyond anything I could imagine. Her son was seventeen at the time of the shooting. His killer was also seventeen. Caught, he was tried as an adult, convicted, and sentenced to life in prison.

Every month, this man who killed receives an unusual visitor. It is the mother of his victim. She brings him cookies and the flower of her love. She has forgiven him not only with her mouth but with her actions. She knows his remorse and regret and she absorbs that with him, offering the fragrance of her forgiveness.

Is this what we mean by love? This mother is certainly a shining example worthy, some might say, of some kind of sainthood.

But is this an isolated story? From Liverpool, England, comes a second harrowing report. Anthony Walker, a kind and gifted eighteen-year-old, was murdered in 2005 by two men who hated the color of his skin. When asked by a reporter how she felt about the men convicted of killing her son, Gee Walker, Anthony's grief-stricken mother, said: "Do I forgive them? At the point of death Jesus said, 'I forgive them because they do not know what they do'. I have got to forgive them. I still forgive them."

If these two mothers can forgive their son's killers, what are *we* called to do in our everyday lives? Caregivers carry enough challenges. To ask them to forgive the many people who may be unkind to them across a week may seem like too big a request.

Yet there is a surprise in all of this.

Forgiveness brings not only relief, but grace. Consider the burden of hatred and the poison of revengeful thinking. What does this do to the heart of the one who hates? The women who forgave their son's killers find that they live with love and grace. They celebrate the sons they had and now seek to do the unthinkable: to spread the fragrance of their love to the men who crushed the lives of their sons.

The caregiver who forgives, in her or his heart, the angry patient, the rude family member, the inconsiderate supervisor, is the one who moves through the world with a lighter and more loving heart. The forgiving caregiver frees him- or herself of the burden of hostility.

Love's Atomic Power: In 1905, one of the great geniuses of history discovered the formula for the physics of energy. Einstein developed his theory from his understanding that every object, inanimate or otherwise, contained enormous reserves of energy that had the potential to release quantum amounts of power.

Here in the 21st century, we have the chance to make an equally important discovery. More powerful than $E=mc^2$ is the discovery that $L=hc^2$. Love is the power of humanity multiplied by compassion squared. The compassion of forgiveness releases an explosion of love's energy through us, an energy which is healing for those who give as well as those who receive. This is the formula of Jesus, the greatest genius of love the world has ever seen.

REFLECTIVE PRACTICE

Before the sun sets on this day, find someone to forgive. Begin by forgiving *yourself* for something. Then forgive the other starting in your heart. Let the voice of forgiveness speak through you. There is no question that other voices will speak against love. The dark angel within you will call you a fool for considering kindness toward an enemy. "Why should you forgive him or her?" the voice will scream. "Look what they did to you. If you forgive, you will be endorsing bad behavior, won't you?"

And in this last question comes one of the other learnings about forgiveness. To forgive does not mean to approve. Each of us must take responsibility for the ways we break trust with others. Forgiveness begins by taking responsibility for our own mistakes and then letting go of shame and revenge.

To err is human. To err against another is also human. To seek revenge is to hate. To forgive is to love. Forgiveness is an act of grace, not of pity. And forgiveness grows a garden full of violets whose fragrance heals the hearts of lovers.

THE PHYSICS OF LOVE

There is more potential power in a single human spirit than in any atom bomb.

—E.C.

On August 6, 1945, the world learned of the stunning power that could explode from a single object when an atomic bomb was dropped on Hiroshima, Japan. How could such extensive devastation arise from such a relatively small metal tube? How could a bomb smaller than a typical room destroy all the rooms in almost all the houses in the city?

It doesn't take a physics major to understand the raw mathematical result: 100,000 people killed in seconds.

And we don't need to be expert scientists to appreciate Einstein's insight that enormous energy is locked up inside even the tiniest mass, an energy made evident when that mass is multiplied by the speed of light squared.

What energy is locked up inside a human being? How can caregivers make use of their enormous power to mix love with the tools of medicine to create healing?

Nuclear power can be put to good or hostile use depending upon the decision of the human beings that manage that power. The power of love lives in each of us and in groups of people as well. What kind of energy does it take for a single person or a few to awaken the power of millions of people?

We all know that a single human being, smaller in physical size than an atomic bomb, was able to awaken enough hatred to kill millions. That's the kind of poisonous energy Adolph Hitler awakened amid the devastated economy of Germany in the 1930s. I don't know that he killed a single person himself. Yet it was his horrible power to persuade that awakened a killing hatred in the minds of millions of Germans.

Joseph Stalin did the same thing during his evil rule of the Soviet Union. Millions met their deaths in Siberian prison camps, all on the orders that came from the mouth of that single twisted soul.

In contemporary times, millions more meet their deaths because of a force stronger than the atomic bomb. Hatred led to the killing of hundreds of thousands in Rwanda. Hundreds of thousands more have died in Darfur and other parts of Africa as the bombs of hatred explode across the world.

These examples illustrate the quantum effect of hatred. What about the quantum effect of Love? What single soul has awakened love in the minds of billions? Christians look to Jesus as the source that planted and nourished the seed of love across the world. Moslems look to the life of Mohammed. Others look to Confucius or Moses or Buddha.

Jesus moved through his short earthly life as a single being so deeply infused with God's love that he was able to plant seeds of hope that have bloomed in countless hearts. His solitary life, his words, and his sacrifice offer love's energy to today's world two thousand years after his crucifixion. Through the example of his one life, we can feel the power that positive energy holds to heal our deepest wounds.

The revelation in all of this is that each of us is capable of awakening healing in others by how we engage the power of love. Consider not only Martin Luther King Jr., but all the people who followed him. Consider not only the life of Mother Teresa, but all those who have been inspired by the example of this one tiny soul from Albania. Consider Gandhi and the millions that followed this powerful little man who, dressed in the simplest cotton wrap, stood as a shining example of peace and nonviolence. Each of these was a single soul. Each generated more power than any atom bomb.

Reflect, now, on the power a single caregiver can have on the life of a single patient, a family, a group of the patient's friends. Nashville physicians Keith Hagan, Cheryl Fassler, Liz Krueger, and Roy Elam are four doctors I know whose healing powers go far beyond the tools they wield or the medicines they prescribe. These doctors create healing by weaving loving care into their ministrations to patients. This means that their patients receive a benefit that patients of less-caring doctors do not receive. Each of them has touched the lives of thousands. Any doctor can integrate love into his or her care. Many don't. These four do. And in so doing, they change the lives of the patients they treat.

The same is true of nurses like Deadre Hall, Laura Madden, and Lorraine Eaton. They are but three examples of thousands of nurses across America who spin a halo of healing around their patients by the way they give loving care.

Each caregiver has the opportunity to do this every day. The question becomes how to find this energy and release it in caregiving? The answer is that this power can flow through each of us when we slide our egos out of the way and let love shine through our hearts to fill the needs of others.

Small atom bombs can wreak havoc across giant cities. Individual human beings can spread the massive power of love across the entire world of caregiving. Each of us can release the explosive energy of love in our lives. There is more potential power in a single human spirit than in any atom bomb.

THE TEARS OF THINGS

...crying is healthy. It is the twin emotion of laughter.

—Dr. Linda E. Jordan

Enchanted as I am with poetic language, I could not resist seeking out the genesis of Lucretius's phrase, the "Tears of Things," when I saw it referenced by poet Robert Bly in one of his essays. In the course of tracking this phrase, I found, on the Internet, an exceptional essay on the role of tears in caregiving. It is by Dr. Linda E. Jordan, Manager of Duke Community Bereavement Services, part of Duke Community Care. Dr. Jordan's brief essay is a brilliant commentary on the respect we need to offer to the unusually visible way that our grief may express itself—if we let it.

I offer Dr. Jordan's one-page reflection in its entirety. My hope is that it may influence us in our work—not to discourage tears, but to recognize and honor them as "part of love" and a "part of healing." This essay may forever change the way you give care.

The Tears of Things

That wonderful Latin phrase, *lacrimae rerum* ("the tears of things"), by Lucretius, is worth contemplating. As a grief counselor, I am used to tears. In fact, Kleenex is my stock in trade. I measure my day's success by how many boxes of tissue are used. One of the most important aspects of my work is to make a safe place for people to cry.

For the most part, we are ashamed of tears. They embarrass us, and most tragically, we view them as a sign of weakness. We hate to cry because it messes up our appearance. Tears make us vulnerable. Some people fear that if they allow themselves to start crying, they will never stop (though they will). Others fear that their emotions will be discounted and belittled. Tears are scary for the person crying.

Tears are also scary for those who witness the tears. We think it is our job to "stop" the tears. We try to console with trite and often hurtful platitudes in an effort to soothe the pain. It never works. Our motives may be kind, but our efforts merely reinforce the idea that tears are bad; they are to be avoided. We praise people for "holding up so well." Our discomfort

in the midst of obvious and palpable pain speaks loudly: "For God's sake, don't cry in front of me; I can't take it." Maybe we secretly fear the tears of others because they call forth so many "tears of things" stored up in our own lives that have long gone unexpressed. Well, I would like to suggest two radical attitudes about crying. These are not original insights. As always, they come from my teachers—grieving people.

First, crying is healthy. It is the twin emotion of laughter. In fact, only those things that evoke profound joy can evoke profound tears. And one of the precious gifts we can give is our undivided and uninterrupted attention to the tears of others. I learned this lesson years ago when I was a chaplain in the Air Force. I was among the first females to serve as a military chaplain. My counseling popularity with young airmen was very gratifying; however, I falsely supposed it was due to my superb counseling skills. In reality, it had to do with my gender. I represented for them a safe place to let down their guard and cry.

This insight came to me one day when a young airman came into my office, introduced himself, sat down, and launched wholeheartedly into spilling out his heart and "the tears of things." At the end of the hour, the airman stood up, thanked me for all my help, and left. I never said a word. I didn't even get the chance to introduce myself. No need. What I learned that day was that helping people cry is not a passive, helpless act. Tears are not only good for our souls, but also good for our bodies. The physical release of tears, like the sweat that comes when we exercise, is cleansing. (There is, after all, more room on the outside than on the inside.) The more at ease we are with tears (ours and others), the more healing we offer. People don't need advice. Most people have the answers they need within them. What they need is presence and safety.

Second, crying is an expression of love. The story that prompted me to write this article came from a woman whose husband died in hospice. She said that as they approached his death, she cried when she was with him. Her son suggested that they should not be so emotional in front of him. They needed to be strong for him, to set their own feelings aside. This wise woman one day asked her husband of 52 years, "When I cry, do I look weak?" Her equally wise husband replied, "When you cry, it looks like love to me." All too often our efforts to "protect" leave those we love more isolated in their pain. "WHEN YOU CRY, IT LOOKS LIKE LOVE TO ME!" What a great alternative consciousness for our culture.

Well, the "tears of things" are part of life. They are part of death. They are part of love. They are part of healing. They are part of remembering. And they are part of moving forward. Bless them, for they are the ultimate gift of our deepest humanity.

GENTLENESS BORN OF WISDOM

13 Who is wise and understanding among you? Show by your good life that your works are done with gentleness born of wisdom...17 But the wisdom from above is first pure, then peaceable, gentle, willing to yield, full of mercy and good fruits... (James 3:13,17)

A nd what is this *wisdom* that gives birth to our gentler nature? In the next chapter of his letter, James quotes the answer:

> God opposes the proud
> but gives grace to the humble.

It is in humility that we find grace and with it the gentleness and compassion we need to be loving caregivers.

All of us are born with some level of aggression. We are filled with endless desires to fill our own needs. That is why we need James, among others, to remind us to let go of our desires. Conflicts and disputes "come from [our] cravings" he warns us. But we cannot simply stop craving, can we?

Instead, we need to think of how we may free ourselves from needless internal and external struggles by surrendering to God's love. We see the grace of this surrender in the cycles of nature. Summer does not seek to force itself into fall. Winter doesn't pursue victory over spring. In each season, we see the surrender of the earth to whatever may befall her, glorying in fertility, suffering in drought, accepting her fate with grace.

Yet we are humans. We carry both the divine spark and the ability to yield to our darkest desires. We have been handed not only bodies with appetites, but egos laced with desires. Our egos stir us to pride. Our divine spark calls us to love.

Does this mean that our lives must be suffused with struggle? The answer seems to be that the challenge of desire falls unequally among us. Some are flooded with deep longings that overpower them. Others are blessed with the wisdom to resist the darkest calls of the world and choose light.

Clerics tell us that faith is a key part of the answer. We can also take heart from the wisdom of Lincoln who called us simply to listen to "the

better angels of our nature."

The dynamics of desire hold paradox. The more we resist desire, the greater desire's pull seems to be—as if we are handing power to craving but trying to deny it.

Where attention goes, energy flows. As we redirect our energy to the voices of our better angels, their voices come to dominate our lives diluting the poison of choices that would harm others. Choosing light becomes easier when we focus our attention on loving others.

Each of us has the chance to "show by [our] good life that [our] works are done by gentleness born of wisdom." We know this wisdom. As care-givers, it's the *practice* of this wisdom that matters to our patients, their loved ones, and our team members. As we live love, fear recedes. This is God's gift to us—to live in love, not in fear.

QUANTUM CAREGIVING

Caregivers chronically underestimate their ability to be agents of healing as well as curing.

—E.C. ,

One of our finest popular thinkers on healing is the physician and writer Deepak Chopra. Dr. Chopra's insights can help us understand how we, as caregivers, can engage the energy of love in healing. This does not mean that *we* become healers, but that we may become *agents* of healing.

Dr. Chopra has said, "What has surprised me most is that when given insight, even a little bit of insight, patients find themselves empowered to do the impossible."

Caregivers who have learned the gift of presence can awaken healing in others. This is part of the gift of not Quantum self-healing, but a new phrase for something ancient: *Quantum Caregiving*. We have the ability to help redirect energy in others as well as in ourselves. The best caregivers engage in a lovely choreography with patients that converts what was once seemed "impossible" into a healing reality.

Quantum healing, according to Chopra, "involves healing one mode of consciousness, mind, to bring about changes in another mode of consciousness, body."

I have often used the famous example of Norman Cousins's astonishing recovery from a "terminal" connective tissue disease as an illustration of our ability to self-heal by redirecting our energy. Cousins directed his energy into humor. Somehow, this appeared to dissipate the toxicity of his illness and, against all of his doctors' prognoses, Cousins recovered.

Quantum Caregiving, different from quantum healing, involves directing our loving energy towards *others* and helping awaken in them their ability to heal. This does not automatically mean that disease goes away. Healing is about more than curing. Quantum Caregiving has to do with engaging and promoting the well-being of the entire other, not just their diseased part.

We all know people who have been cured but are not healed. In the same way, we know people with cancer who are healed, but not cured.

Quantum Caregiving, among other things, seeks to approach, with respect, the toxic energy of certain attitudes in both ourselves and others. Stress is attitudinally based and can be healed. When Mr. Cousins started his pattern of daily "laugh therapy," we can assume that his stress level went down. Scientists now know that stress affects our T-cell count and our body's ability to fight infection. This is an important thing for healing caregivers to know as they approach others—that their job is not only to fix what is broken but to help awaken in the other their ability to self-heal.

The core of Quantum Caregiving is the approach it takes toward the spirit. Curing aims at correcting physical illness. Caring address the spirit. Curing tends to approach the body as a machine. Quantum Caregiving appreciates the human body as a place touched by the divine spirit.

It requires significant reflection, prayer, and meditation to appreciate the potential of Quantum Caregiving. We all know about those who administer it—the well-known, Jesus, St. Francis, Mother Teresa—and the lesser-known like the nurse or social worker down the hallway who brings a healing spirit to caregiving and, almost miraculously, often gains healing results with patients.

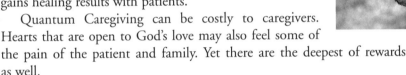

Quantum Caregiving can be costly to caregivers. Hearts that are open to God's love may also feel some of the pain of the patient and family. Yet there are the deepest of rewards as well.

Some believe that Jesus' ability to bring about physical healing may have distracted people from his primary goal: to heal souls, not bodies. The evidence for this is in his occasional requests that individuals he had healed not tell anyone of what he had done. Yet he also felt the need to demonstrate the power of God's love in ways that were visible to doubting humans.

Modern American hospitals have become obsessed with patient satisfaction surveys. Did the patient seem to like how they were treated by staff? These surveys have their place. But of far deeper importance is not surface satisfaction but a deeper sense of being more healed by a sacred encounter with a caregiver. This is the power of Quantum Caregiving. It begins with a caregiver's awareness that their specific presence, something that arises from the heart, can have a great impact. A loving heart shows itself in everything from voice tone and body language to the deepest kind of listening and affirming presence.

I have applied a strange-sounding phrase, Quantum Caregiving, to something many people have been doing in their work for years. By using this phrase, I hope to make you even more aware of something you may sense about yourself. That you have your own God-given ability to be a channel of light and love to all those around you.

THE MEANING EFFECT

It is the human commitment to high purpose that can brighten and change our world.

—E.C.

We all know the phenomenon. A certain number of patients in research studies designed to test new drugs will recover from their illness even though they are in a control group that is only taking a so-called "sugar pill" or some other harmless substance. The notion is that these patients are getting better because they *believe* they are taking some magical new treatment.

It turns out the placebo effect is the wrong way to describe the quantum impact of this phenomenon. What the studies prove is the role our *belief* has on our body's ability to recover. Drs. Daniel Moerman and Wayne Jones believe, therefore, that we should rename this process "The Meaning Effect."

The great Dr. Viktor Frankl would probably have preferred that we call it the "Purpose Effect" based on his discovery that there was a direct relationship between the purposefulness of concentration camp victims and their ability to survive.

What these thinkers are telling us is something we know but underestimate. Belief affects healing. This is also part of the theory I advance called *Quantum Caregiving*. When caregivers accept and live out the understanding of the power of the human mind and spirit to heal itself, they become partners in sacred encounters with their patients, not simply robots administering drugs.

The existing patterns in the American medical-industrial complex do little to support caregivers in this approach. It will take at least a generation for Quantum Caregiving to be practiced as well as understood. We know how to hand people pills. We are less clear about the kind of presence we can offer that can have a different and more powerful impact than any medication.

You and I have seen this phenomenon many times. I saw it recently at Alive Hospice in Nashville as a mother climbed into bed with her dying eight-year old son to catch his tears, to comfort him, to hand him the gift of her love. When Ginger, the boy's nurse, saw what was happening,

she backed away. "He needs his mother at a time like this, not me." What a beautiful recognition on Ginger's part of the healing power of a mother's love.

A housekeeper stops to comfort the confusion of an elderly patient crying out for his absent daughter. And in her touch, she brings relief and, for a time, healing. A nurse strokes the back of a dying baby. She has no medicine to cure him. But instead of abandoning the baby's case as hopeless, she loves him on his final journey out of this world. Another housekeeper at another hospital sings Amazing Grace to ease the pain of a patient. An operating room nurse holds up the entire schedule to give a blind wife the chance to hear her husband's voice one more time before surgeons remove his cancer-ridden voice box forever.

All of these are examples of Quantum Caregiving. Each of them reflects the impact of the Meaning Effect. These are not examples of curing, they are expressions of the gift of loving care—of healing beyond curing.

QUESTIONS

- How do you interpret the Meaning Effect in your work versus the Placebo Effect?

- Is Quantum Caregiving a phrase you find useful in describing the exponential impact some caregivers have on patients or is it too confusing?

THE TOUCH CARD OF REMEMBRANCE

The most difficult command in the Bible may be: "be still and know that I am God."

—Dr. James Hudnut-Beumler, Dean,
Vanderbilt Divinity School

We know why this command is difficult because we know about all the noise of the world. Can we find a way to hold a silence within as the world shouts at us from highways, televisions, cell phones, pagers, and the second floor?

Here are the words we may hear if we are still. They arrive across the millennia from *Deuteronomy*: "You shall love the Lord your God with all your heart, and with all your soul, and with all your might." These words are so important that we are called to "Bind them as a sign on your hand, fix them as an emblem on your forehead, and write them on the doorposts of your house."

Observant Jews have a lovely way of observing this injunction. On the doorposts of their homes they place a little rectangular case. Inside is a Mezuzah—a bit of parchment reciting the oneness of God. Upon entering and leaving the house, the custom is to touch the Mezuzah as a reminder.

The wisdom in this is the understanding that humans need reminders. Amid all the rules and guidelines of the Bible, Dean Hudnut-Beumler tells us that all we need to remember is this commandment plus the words of Jesus in *Matthew* 22. Together, they bring us the most important wisdom we may need, to love God and to love our neighbors as ourselves.

From the Jewish tradition of touching the Mezuzah, caregivers may adopt an idea of tremendous potential value. I have invited all hospitals, starting with those in the St. Joseph Health System, and spreading across the country, and all hospices, nursing homes, and other charities, to adopt a new *Touch Card* system. The touch card would be placed on or near the door of each patient room. Upon approaching a room, each caregiver would be encouraged to touch the card before entering, like a knock on the door of the soul, a reminder of the sacred humanity of the person in the bed.

It's a small thing, and it can be transformative because it sends a signal throughout the hospital or any charity that uses the touch card: the other person has holiness within. Respect this holiness.

Try the touch card system yourself. Create some small image that is a holy reminder for you of the need to love others. Place this near a threshold you often cross so that your hand may touch it and your heart may be reminded of the stillness within, of the love of God, and of how we express our love of God through loving others.

And now, observe the Sabbath by recalling, again, the wisdom of the Bible: "Be still and know that I am God."

A Hidden Holiness

Often a Holy Thing is living hidden in a dark creature;
and like an eye which is born covered by its lids,
a pure spirit is growing strong under the bark of stones!

—Gerard de Nerval, 1854 (translated by Robert Bly)

I t's easy to see beauty in roses, in blue skies, in sapphire seas. With people, we argue our various ideas of what is cute and make icons of the handsome and the pretty, particularly if they are young.

Caregivers, however, are accustomed to confronting people the rest of us may seek to avoid: the homeless, the elderly, and people of all ages whose disease may steal from them the appearance of what we think of as beautiful. I admire the courage of caregivers who labor in the midst of blood, pain, and tragedy. Each of us hopes to be cared for by angels of compassion and competence should we suddenly find our bodies wrecked by an accident or burned by fire. It is then that we may see the embrace of loving arms. We want to be loved by someone who appreciates the many sides of our vulnerability.

Everyone enjoys the story *Beauty and the Beast*. Yet few may see the application of this story to caregiving. Everyone who chooses to care for illness with deep grace and respect is given the opportunity to see the beauty hidden beneath ugly surfaces. When they replace revulsion with compassion, they reveal beauty in themselves and, sometimes, in the people they treat.

The Matthew Walker Clinic is the largest service of its kind that cares for the poor in Nashville. For whom do they care? I've seen their waiting room filled with the tired faces of the poor who, in addition to their burdens, have often spent much of their lives waiting in many different kinds of lines to be served by many different agencies. The poor are cursed by endless waiting for things the rest of us often acquire more easily.

It is the challenge of compassionate caregivers to hear the story that lives within the sick body, to see past the injury to the human being, for there is always more than just the physical pain. When we come for care, we hurt. Each of brings at least two kinds of "hurts."

A twelve-year-old girl was brought to the Clinic recently with an ugly problem. Raped by her father, she is now pregnant. Her body has been vio-

lated and her heart has been hurt. This is a story none of us wants to hear. The job of the caregivers is to open their arms—to offer compassion, not pity, to offer support, not judgment. A nurse named Pat and a doctor named Williams will be two of this girl's angels. They are veterans of dealing with ugly problems, but their hearts have not been hardened. They know that a "Holy Thing" lives hidden somewhere in this darkness. Inside this tragedy live human spirits.

There are other kinds of darkness loving caregivers face. At a rural clinic, a large and menacing young man climbs off his motorcycle, charges into the waiting area, and confronts a nurse manager. He is angry, he is shouting, his fists are clinched. What does a loving caregiver do? Most would order the man to sit down and *quiet* down. But this caregiver did a wonderfully compassionate thing. She looked up at the man, a foot taller than she, and said softly, "You must have had a hard day." All the man's

anger evaporated. In an instant, the nurse manager revealed the holy hiding in the darkness. She saw that beneath this man's anger was fear. Speaking to that, she converted his hostility to warmth as he sat down, put his head in his hands, and apologized. Beauty's love transformed the beast in this man.

Today, thousands of kind-hearted caregivers will reveal the holy hidden in the darkness. They will see good where others see only bad, they will meet hostility and ugliness with grace and compassion. And thousands of others will stay imprisoned in harsher views of their patients. They will argue with the sick, grumble about low pay, and complain about the many messes they must clean up.

It is not for us to judge. Caregiving is hard work, but it need not be dreary. This is what the best caregivers know. They approach their work with gratitude for the chance to help others and find light in darkness.

It is for us to love, support, and care for every caregiver we can. We may also offer our prayers and hope that our own eyes may remain open to see that within each person "a pure spirit is growing strong under the bark of stones."

Today I invite your presence to reflect with gratitude on all caregivers who have found the grace to see with sacred eyes, to approach sickness with courage and competence, and to open their hearts to embrace the pain of others. These are the angels around us. I invite you to celebrate their beautiful willingness to be present to darkness.

TRUSTING LOVE

Truly I tell you, whoever does not receive the kingdom of God as a little child will never enter it. (Mark 10:15)

When I first heard this scripture long ago, I thought it meant, literally, that if you didn't receive God as a little kid, you were done for. I felt badly for all those old folks in distant parts of the world that didn't seem to have caught God and how it was too late for them now. As a child, I liked the images in church windows and paintings of Jesus welcoming us.

It took me a while to appreciate that Jesus was saying, instead, that as adults we needed to regain the innocent openness of little children in order to appreciate God's kingdom. Society teaches us sophistication and orders us to follow its rules. Society also teaches us a vast range of fears.

Psychologists know that we are born with only two fears: of falling and of loud noises (startle reflexes). It is the fear of falling that Alfred Hitchcock understood so well, as so many of his movies, from *Vertigo* to *North by Northwest*, exploit this fear.

What is important, here, is that life teaches us fear. Some versions of faith teach fear of God rather than love. And yet Jesus invites us to return to the open innocence of childhood to receive God's kingdom. We must find the courage to let go of the things of this world. We must regain trust.

Why is it hard for us to trust? We have, of course, been betrayed many times. And each betrayal has left a scar, and a memory of how painful it was to "lose" something or someone.

As adults, we are called to reach beneath all of these scars, to stride through the many curtains of our remembered wounds, to conquer our fear by trusting God with the purity and certainty of an infant in the arms of a mother's love.

Life teaches us to fight. Jesus calls us to surrender, to trust with the innocence of children.

What does this trust look like in adult behavior? When Mother Teresa chose to enter the slums of Calcutta to care for the poorest of the poor, many thought she was a fool and ridiculed her. Undeterred by this criticism, she stated, "I am following Christ where He is leading me."

When Rosa Parks chose to keep her seat in the back of a Montgomery bus, she trusted God, not the angry bus driver who ordered her to stand. When Gandhi patiently received the physical blows of angry policemen, he was listening to God's voice, not the world's.

Caregivers know that each time they feel themselves letting go of their will and following God's, they experience a glimmer of God's love. And each time they trust as children, the door to the kingdom slides open another inch.

This doesn't mean caregivers are free of betrayal and protected from wounds. The world will always wound those who trust. It means that God blesses those who trust in love with sincere intention.

There will always be those who ridicule the lovers of this world. "You fool!" they will shout to someone who puts aside his or her own safety and comfort to meet the needs of another—whether it's the man who, in the  middle of a cold night, gives up his coat to warm a stranger or the nurse who sits for long stretches with an Alzheimer's patient or the caregiver who offers lovingkindness to a rude and angry patient.

"Why bother?" some will say. And the answer is that this is how lovers behave. This is what it looks like to offer our love knowing, sometimes with certainty, that we will be betrayed. This is what it is to trust like a child with the courage of an adult. To love God more than this world.

Catching Tears

Compassion is not administered in cubic centimeters from a syringe but is found in a river of love that flows from the heart.

—E.C.

She crosses the threshold of the Siloam Clinic in Nashville holding a washcloth against the side of her face. She is from Guatemala and speaks no English. A caregiver sees her slumped in the waiting room. "Does she have a toothache?" he worries, because there are no dentists at the Clinic. "Has she received a blow to the face in an auto accident?" he wonders next.

He approaches her. Through a translator, the caregiver learns something stunning. *Why* the washcloth? "It is to catch my tears," the woman says in Spanish.

Abused by her husband, this woman has no visible physical wounds, but her sadness is intense, deep, and beyond any translation that uses words. The Siloam Clinic does an amazingly wonderful job of caring for all kinds of health problems that afflict their largely immigrant patient population. How do they treat sadness, especially when there is the barrier of language?

As the Loving Care movement continues to advance across the nation, there are increasing challenges that threaten to sidetrack the movement. One of the biggest is convincing measurement-obsessed leaders that the delivery of compassion is a critical part of healing care. The temptation is to denigrate compassion as, at best, a nice little "customer service" extra and, at worst, useless.

This is a tragic mistake. Compassion is essential because most patients come for care hurting in many different ways. Physical care addresses only one need of the patient. Customer service is a crude notion transferred from the world of department stores that assumes the patient has come to buy a commodity. Customer service is woefully inadequate in addressing the challenge of a patient's grief. What patients seek, the thing we want for our loved ones and ourselves, is *loving* service.

Compassion is not administered in cubic centimeters from a syringe but is found in a river of love that flows from the heart.

So how do Siloam caregivers do it? They are inspired by the scripture from the Gospel of John about Jesus healing at the Pool of Siloam, and they follow the principles outlined in our books, *Radical Loving Care* and *Sacred Work*. Among other things, they pay exquisite attention to the *hiring* process. As a faith-based charity, they *orient* staff to "see the face of Christ" in each patient. They spend time praying with patients who wish the *presence* of prayer. Leaders there, starting with CEO Nancy West and new Medical Director Jim Henderson, M.D., follow the practice of *caring for the people who care for people*. And they regularly *invite* staff into *caring conversation circles* to help enhance all the dimensions of caregiving.

As a result, Siloam, with a beautiful mix of paid staff and caring volunteers, offers loving care that is perfectly balanced with competence and compassion. The tearful woman from Guatemala receives not just medical support, but the engagement of a social worker, the presence of a chaplain,

and the warm embrace of the loving arms of all of the Siloam staff. The staff learns the patient's story. They don't see this patient as "that Guatemalan woman," they see her as a child of God and they treat her with respect, skill, and profound presence.

Why can't all hospitals and charities do the same thing? They can. And they needn't be faith-based to bring love into each encounter. Why don't most organizations run like this? Because there is an inadequate appreciation of how important compassion is to the caregiving process.

We have spoken about the exponential impact a caregiver can have if she or he approaches a patient's need with love instead of treating it as a commercial-style transaction. Healing caregivers can release curative energy in their patients in a way that, if we could see it on a screen, would be as powerful as an atomic reaction. Atomic power engages a process we call chain reactions so that huge responses can flow from inside tiny particles of energy.

The same is true with loving care. Healing energy can flow from the touch of a hand, the quiet presence of a caring social worker, the prayer of a pastor. The woman from Guatemala received these gifts, and the weight of her sadness has been eased. The staff caught her tears and helped convert them to joy.

This woman entered the clinic crushed by sadness. She left with new hope and a smile on her face. Does this matter? What if this woman was your sister, your mother, your daughter, your friend?

CAMELS, NEEDLES AND LOVE

It is easier for a camel to go through the eye of a needle than for someone who is rich to enter the kingdom of God. (Mark 10:25)

The middle and upper economic classes hate this statement from Jesus. I got to feeling so guilty about my own wealth a few years ago that I considered giving most of what I have away. For a while, the idea seemed enchanting (my wife, understandably, was less enthusiastic).

Of course, I didn't do anything—except to increase my contributions to charity and to become more active in working to help the poor and vulnerable. I suppose this is the best most of us do. We've worked so hard for our money and the stuff it buys that the idea of parting with it seems not only hard but foolish. Yet all the way back to the prophet Amos we have been admonished to help the poor.

So what is Jesus asking of us? The literal part is clear enough. We are asked to get rid of, or give away, our money and our stuff. At another level, the call is to free ourselves from attachment to material things. Most Buddhists do a better job at this than most Christians. They understand what Jesus understood. Acquiring things can bring out some pretty unchristian behavior: possessiveness, lawsuits, wars to protect our turf and our possessions.

There's a myth out there that new things bring happiness. Sometimes they do for a few hours or a few days, but then what? Does the new car have a little dent? Is there a tear in that new shirt? Is the new boat already seeming less fun?

The most reliable studies show that there is no meaningful difference in happiness levels between a person making $50,000 per year and people making $1,000,000 per year. However, there *is* a difference between people making $50,000 per year and people living below the poverty line.

This is the challenge of true charity. The poor walk the earth today. In some parts of the world, sub-Saharan Africa for example, eight- and ten-year-olds are sent to work pounding rocks into fine dust for concrete. It takes two weeks' work to get enough dust to fill a bag sold for $3—barely enough for subsistence.

By Jesus' guideline (if it were the only one), the eye of the needle will grow as large as a palace door for these poor children, all of whom will pass through easy as kings. The arms of heaven will welcome them.

And the arms of heaven would welcome, as well, so many others that suffered in various kinds of poverty across their life journey. These include the vulnerable served by loving charities.

Whether the door to heaven is wide as an elephant or tiny as a needle, the question being asked on the other side of the door is, what is our intention underneath each action we take? Do we act from love or fear?

If we give away everything for the sole purpose of widening the door for ourselves, we may discover that it is closed to us. God is love. The question is not how much we have, but how much of ourselves we will give to meet the needs of others—and with what intention—to help another or ourselves?

How much are we willing to put aside our personal comfort to fill the God-shaped hole in another's heart? Do we come to the table of communion with love of God or with fear for ourselves?

Jesus said we need to become like children, to rediscover trust and innocence. We need to shed as much as we can of the world's stuff and find a way to be as loving and as true as children. As caregivers, we need to find a way to move through this world as lovers—not worried about whether *we* can get into heaven, but whether we can live our lives helping those in need.

YOU ALONE...

And it was then that in the depths of sleep
Someone breathed to me: "You alone can do it,
Come immediately."

—Jules Supervielle (translated by Geoffrey Gardner)

We spend about a third of our lives in sleep and part of that time in the strange land of dreams. The late Uruguayan-born poet Jules Supervielle (1884-1960) left us many beautiful lines of poetry and prose. The above three lines from the end of his poem "The Call" provoke memories of times when we have heard voices in the quiet of the night, perhaps in dreams, possibly in half-awake moments when suddenly we hear a voice calling to us. We raise up on our elbow, look about, realize that the voice was probably coming from within. What do these secret voices breathe to us? *What is it that we alone can do?*

This is the most personal of questions and one of the most important ones for us to ask ourselves. So much of what we do in our work may be done by others just as well or better. What are the unique things that we alone may bring to the table of love—things that are special to our own hearts?

I have sometimes heard the cynical voice of some leaders say, "everyone is replaceable." The better truth is, everyone's *job* is replaceable, but no *person* is replaceable. We each hold the potential to do as poet David Whyte calls us to do: *bring our hearts to work.* When we do this, we are bringing the most special element of our lives into the work place.

There is something we alone can do. We can bring our own version of love to the bedside of a patient, to the meeting table, to any encounter we have with someone in need.

There is, of course, a counter force, a two-word question that represents the center of cynicism. It comes from those who look at any given act with the lazy inquiry, "So what?"

Loving caregivers need never wonder about the answer to this question. Every kind act is meaningful, whether we see the consequences of that act or not. Each loving gesture sends a ripple of light into the world.

On this day, we may ask what special secret we hold within us: What voice breathes to us that we must bring our uniqueness to someone

immediately? The voice is strange, and yet we know it. There is always someone who needs us, whether they speak the need out loud or not.

Find the person that needs you. Go to them. Share your love with them today in a way only you can. So that at the end of this day, in the middle of the night as you lie in the land of dreams, you may hear a voice breathing to you in the depths of your sleep: "Thank you for your gift of love."

SECRETS

Some of our most beautiful secrets are unknown even to us.

—E.C.

Whom we think of the secrets within us, we may imagine that all of them are dark. But our hearts hold secrets we have yet to discover that are bright and beautiful. We need to listen to the voice of these secrets to enable them to find a home outside of us as gifts to this world. We need to be present to the lovely secrets that sit quietly within us.

Every so often someone will say to me: "People are either kind or not, so you can't *teach* people to love." Is this really true? Are people either lovers or haters? Almost everyone I know is somewhere in-between. Most people can be kind to those they know and love and have an almost equal capability to be mean towards those they feel are threatening.

I've seen this in emergency departments. Once I watched a clerk in the middle of a harsh exchange with a patient. Suddenly a friendly fellow-worker appeared. In a flash, the clerk's scowl flipped to a smile, "Hi Judy, how are you doing?"

This chameleon capability of ours is cause for hope when reflecting on loving care. We hold many secret powers within us. These secrets, when revealed, can bring some wonderful surprises.

We know, for example, that the same clerk who smiled at her friend could turn that beautiful, powerful smile on the patient in front of her. As Martin Luther King Jr. said with typical wisdom, eloquence, and insight, "The only way to turn an enemy into a friend is with love."

I've been trying to follow my own advice recently in connection with a long-time competitor who shows every sign of hating me. I know that he has spoken unkindly about me to others and that he has even sought to block my presence in the organization he runs. When he does these things, what should I do? As a trained trial lawyer, I am tempted to use the weapons of argument, threat, and attack. But of what value are these tools as expressions of love?

Contrary to popular belief, it is possible for lawyers to use their gifts of argument in loving ways—for example, to help the poor and to strive for

justice. Yet, in this case, the issue is primarily one of ego between this man and me. The best answer is to live love, not fear or anger.

So I have set upon a path of unilateral acts of kindness. I have asked him for forgiveness for any wrong I've done and I've offered gifts. Thus far, this has generated no change in his response. But perhaps the goal is not to change him but to release a secret power from within me—the power to forgive without expectation of anything in return. I can tell you that, frankly, I feel better responding to him with love than I would trying to plot ways to undercut him. Is this a secret power that lies within you as well?

The Ukrainian poet Anna Akhmatova (1889–1966) offers us twelve beautiful lines that, if we allow them to enter our hearts, may lift us above the petty and the mundane. Through her words, we may transcend trouble for a moment and reflect on the many beautiful secrets that lie within each of us.

A land not mine, still
forever memorable,
the waters of its ocean
chill and fresh.

Sand on the bottom whiter than chalk,
and the air drunk, like wine,
late sun lays bare
the rose limbs of the pinetrees.

Sunset in the ethereal waves:
I cannot tell if the day
is ending, or the world, or if
the secret of secrets is inside me again.

—Anna Akhmatova (translated by Jane Kenyon)

Perhaps the secret of secrets is within us always. Perhaps it is time for us, as caregivers, to speak some small part of our secret ability to love as we go about the world seeking to be carriers of God's light.

CAREGIVING AND THE ENERGY OF LOSS

If you want to assess the mood of some American males with whom you work or live, check the sports page on Monday morning.

—E.C.

I know there are plenty of exceptions—that millions of men and tens of millions of women couldn't care less about sports. But scan the television screen on Saturday and Sunday afternoons and you will see a fascinating phenomenon. Grown men (and some women) who may otherwise seem sane the rest of the week, who will don suits for work on Monday morning, who would never think of shouting in a business meeting, have actually painted their faces various colors, stripped off their shirts, put feathers in their hair, tattooed their bodies, and done everything they can to imitate savage behavior, including screaming their heads off—all on behalf of their beloved team.

One Saturday afternoon, I watched something very painful for me and any loyal alumnus of Northwestern University. The Wildcats (my team) were ahead 38 to 3 midway through the third quarter against the much stronger and much bigger Michigan State Spartans. Who could lose with that kind of lead? Northwestern, not unlike Vanderbilt (who also lost that Saturday), has a long tradition of loss in football. But their alumni are still loyal. My alma mater even sells mailboxes in the shape of a football helmet.

By halftime, some Spartan fans, convinced no team could overcome such a deficit, were leaving the stadium in disgust. Having watched my team lose so often, I wasn't so sure. There was still a quarter and a half left. And, you guessed it, Michigan State, in the most astonishing comeback I've ever seen in college football, came back to win 41-38 in the final seconds.

What the devil is the relationship between this nonsense and caregiving? I've been wondering for a long time why millions of people worldwide become so fired up about who wins a given game. In almost every case, in almost every major sport I can think of (except ice hockey), the outcome is determined by what people do with some kind of ball and how it's made to move. And yet so many people are so fanatically committed to the outcome of a game that it's common to see fans with their hands together in

prayer during tense moments in the game. Do they supposed that God is carefully weighing the prayers of different fans and deciding the game accordingly?

Game losers are not put to death as sometimes happened in Roman gladiator contests. But from the faces of losers in football, baseball, basketball, or soccer, you'd think someone had died.

With respect to men, the usual explanation from psychologists for their energy and passion around games has something to do with testosterone—the energy this hormone provides to stimulate aggression and the desire to *conquer*. Women, of course, have various amounts of testosterone as well. But, even putting aside this factor, plenty of women seem to develop equally strong attachments to their team—to experience great highs of energy when their team wins and near depression when their team falls.

 The late Vince Lombardi said it: "Winning isn't everything, it's the only thing." Less well-known is the fact that Lombardi said one of his biggest regrets was making this statement. The idea that winning is the *only* thing is one of the most non-Christian, unloving ideas I can imagine. I think Lombardi came to agree with this and that was the cause for his regret.

Human egos can become so blended with a given team or organization that winning and losing becomes personal rather than organizational. Placing so much importance on winning may well be at the root of many of the ethical problems within some American corporations. Worldcom, Enron, HealthSouth come to mind as well as, at one point in the late 1990s, the giant hospital corporation HCA.

Is it because there is so much in life over which we have little influence that sports seems like a harmless way to engage the game of life—to vent some of the aggression we are not allowed to release in other settings?

But what happens to energy when the ego is so identified with a team or a thing (a car?) *or* a relationship that the human being seems depressed in the face of loss? If my body chemistry were measured at the moment my team went down to defeat in a close match, I think it would show a negative change comparable to other kinds of more serious losses in life. Slowly, I'm learning. Hopefully my learning about games is transferring to other, more important, areas of life.

There are valuable teachings about human loss and victory that can be analogized from games to real life.

1) **Competitive Poison:** The leaders of far too many hospitals and charities focus way too much energy on "beating the competition" instead of working to strengthen a culture of loving care in their organization. Part of the reason for this is an excess of male energy in caregiving organizations (whether run by a male or a female). Hospitals and charities are not football teams. They should be dedicated to serving the vulnerable, not to defeating *other* charities.

2) **Indifference:** A typical way to make loss in a game more bearable is to say out loud, "Well, it's just a game." This is a simple technique for regaining perspective and can work when it really is just a football game. But what do people say who have lost a loved one? I've heard some people say, at funerals, "Well, I guess we all die." Common psychological defenses used by many couples when faced with divorce may be lines like, "I never really loved him (or her) anyway." Or, "I always knew he (she) was a rat." Losing a human relationship is painful. Losing a rat sounds like a good thing. It shields us from some of the pain that arises from the betrayal we may be feeling. But adopting an affect of indifference is, ultimately, cold comfort. It can also block us from forming new meaningful relationships to protect our egos and our hearts from any risk of betrayal. When we do this, we turn our backs on some of the richest gifts life has to offer.

3) **Perspective—The Stages of Regaining Balance**: All of this brings us back to the wisdom of the late Elisabeth Kübler-Ross, M.D., who was perhaps the world's leading authority on the grieving process. She identified several stages humans go through when facing loss. All of these apply to the process of *any* loss. Here are the stages again—with my editorial comments connected to game outcomes:

- Denial (This isn't *happening* to me! The referee made a mistake.)

- Anger (Why is this happening to *me*? My team was ahead, how could they lose?)

- Bargaining (I promise I'll be a better person *if*...the video replay shows my team won.)

- Depression (I don't *care* anymore and I'll never watch another game.)

- Acceptance (*I'm ready* for whatever comes. I'm back in balance and have regained my cognitive thinking ability.)

The relevance of Kübler-Ross's stages is the idea that we usually can't skip the first four and land at Acceptance. Healthy grieving requires that we find the courage to work past denial, avoid aiming anger at the innocent other, let go of trying to change the unchangeable through bargaining, find balance in the midst of grieving, and recover the balance that comes from acceptance.

Here comes the Serenity Prayer: *God grant me the courage to accept the things I can't change, the courage to change the things I can, and the wisdom to know the difference.*

All the wisdom to deal with loss (or victory or life itself) is contained in these words.

As a practical matter, however, I would *not* recommend your reading this to someone right after their beloved team loses. Of course not. When people are in the midst of anger or depression, cognitive thinking has little value. People grieving loss, whether of a game or a courtroom trial, or a marriage, don't want lecturing.

What *do* they want? They want one thing from us: *our compassionate presence* (or compassionate *absence* until they can recover). This is what Job wanted from his friends in the face of his suffering. He knew they couldn't solve his problems, he needed (and apparently didn't get) their loving presence.

When I'm upset, I don't want someone else to read the stages of grieving to me and point out what stage I'm in. I want them to listen for what I need, to sympathize with the loss-energy I'm experiencing, perhaps to share the burden. Later on, when I recover, maybe I'll discover that I've been attaching too much importance to a given team or a given thing or even a given relationship.

Caregivers face loss with such frequency that cultivating compassionate presence is of critical importance. Whether it's something that seems as frivolous as a football game or as significant as a cancer diagnosis, the trials of Job, or a death, it's *loving presence* that is the gift that is so often needed.

When someone near us shows the face of defeat and frustration, the truth is they are suffering the toxic energy of loss. Love them by how you are present.

If *you* are the one who is feeling the weight of loss today, may God bless you and bring you the light of love's presence in your suffering.

OUT OF LONELINESS

Who, if I cried out, would hear me among the angels' hierarchies?

—opening to the *Duino Elegies,*
Rainer Maria Rilke (1875–1926)

What do you seek here? Is it comfort? If so, I offer you all the comfort I can from the illumination of this page along with this news: you are loved.

If you seek comfort, I invite you to listen to your breathing, to be present to the air that warms as your body draws it in, holds it, exhales. Breathe in rest. Breathe in comfort

If you seek beauty here, I invite you to look around—to use your sacred eyes and ears.

What do you feel that is beautiful? For beauty is always there, waiting for you to notice her in her various disguises. What do you see now that you have never seen before? Breathe in this discovered beauty with each of your breaths. Exhale into the world your gratitude for this new sight.

If you seek to free yourself of loneliness, you have asked something I cannot answer. I can tell you one person who never seems lonely. He is the sidewalk preacher I see here and there who shouts his sermons into a heedless world. People wandering by are careful to ignore him. Instead, the sidewalk preacher addresses an audience of air. Often, he wears a smile. As if whoever he sees provides all the company, applause, and "Amens" he could ever want. If he never felt heard in his younger years, he seems happy now, listened to by his hierarchy of angels. Perhaps he has an answer that has eluded us.

If I cried out right now, into offices emptied by evening, would anyone hear? If I spoke into a crowd or even to a small circle of friends, or even to you, would I feel heard? If so, would the ghost of loneliness finally flee, replaced by angels carefully weaving me into their quilt of meaning?

Here is the gift for every caregiver. *As we enter the need of another, our loneliness departs.*

Today's poem is nine lines From David Whyte's "The Winter of Listening":

What we strive for
in perfection
is not what turns us
into the lit angel
we desire,

what disturbs us
and then nourishes
has everything
we need.

THE
PRESENCE
MEDITATIONS

INTRODUCTION TO PRESENCE

Someday, after we have mastered the winds, the waves, the tides and gravity, we shall harness for God the energies of love. Then for the second time in the history of the world, we will have discovered fire.

—Teilhard de Chardin

I f there's one thing my two-year-old grandson still understands, it's how to be present. With limited memories in his short life and little to worry about in the future, he knows how to do something many of us have forgotten—he is a living meditation on presence to this moment.

It turns out that the rest of us, with long memories and a preoccupation about the future, need to relearn what we knew when we were two. That is what this collection of meditations is about—relearning presence we once provided naturally as very small children.

The caregiving experience can be among the richest life has to offer. It can also be one of the loneliest, most draining, and most frustrating. The Presence Meditations are for any caregiver and *any* person who desires to be more present to life.

So much depends upon presence. Pause in meditation over how to be present to the power of what is before you *in this moment*. For life is more about everyday elements of beauty than it is about news from Hollywood, what's for sale at the shopping mall, or the latest dispute in Congress.

It's those *other* noisy things that pull us from true presence. It's the sense that there's something else more important than what is happening in front of us right now. Many people fritter away their lives, either dwelling on the past or anticipating the future. In the course of this, they miss the life they are living right now.

A nurse sits with a mother in labor. A counselor sits with a depressed patient. A hospice caregiver sits before a dying patient, a father sits with his small child. Sometimes the temptation is to let the mind drift—to think about the groceries I need to buy on the way home, to review my plans for the weekend, to worry about the incomplete chart waiting at the nurse's station. When I allow my thoughts to drift in such a way, I have lost my presence to the situation before me. And the patient has lost the gift of my presence.

Are we ready yet, as Teilhard de Chardin challenges, to harness for God the energies of love? Indeed, perhaps these energies are not to be harnessed, but to be expressed. Love flows *through* us not *from* us. And when it does, something greater than fire appears. For love brings light.

THREE PRACTICES OF PRESENCE

We were standing on a hill overlooking a great river in northern Ohio called the Maumee. It was 1980. As we watched the current ripple by I said to my mother-in-law, "Marian, I'd love to buy a piece of land along this water."

"That would be nice," she said. "I guess I feel that I already own everything I see."

What a remarkable observation, I thought. We struggle to gain legal possession of things. The greater wisdom is in my mother-in-law's comment. Enjoyment comes from being present to the world before us, not from trying to own it. So much of the world's trouble has come from people trying to take control of territory. Imagine if we turned our attention, instead, to appreciating what is within the reach of our senses and our hearts.

What does it mean to be present to people? It is not much different from being present to the rest of the world around us. We need to allow the door to our souls to slide open.

What are practices that help presence?

PRACTICE 1: QUIETING

The first practice is learning to become *quiet*. Letting ourselves fall silent allows for the noisy demands of the world and our own egos to shrink back, allowing God's light the chance to shine through. I recommend twenty minutes of silent meditation because I find that five is usually not enough. It often takes the first three-fourths of my meditation time for my mind to clear itself and my body to relax. Five minutes is clearly better than nothing. Twenty minutes is better. More than twenty minutes twice a day is not only unrealistic for most caregivers, it may even be counterproductive.

PRACTICE 2: FULL ENGAGEMENT

We need to practice *full engagement*. This starts with the opening of all our senses to the experience before us. If we seek to be present to another, this means full attention. A minister once said to me when our son was small, "Presence is a key part of parenting." I stared back quizzically: "You mean I have to spend a whole lot of time with my son? What about my work?"

"No," he replied, "I'm not talking about quantities of time, I'm talking about the *quality of your presence*. Don't let yourself watch a football game when he's trying to talk to you. Be present to him. Hear him."

PRACTICE 3: SPIRITUAL PRESENCE

Allow your *soul* to be present to the encounter. This is not a mechanical process but a spiritual one. If we are open to the cues offered by another to us, we may begin to see with our *sacred* senses. Consider eye contact. We are taught not to stare. This means we knew how to stare as babies and had to be taught not to do so by society. Anyone who has ever looked into a baby's eyes knows that babies can return our gaze without blinking or turning away. Their eyes are fully open as are they. By sustaining eye contact as a caregiver, we may begin to see more than the information coming to our eyes. At some spiritual level, we may begin to sense much more about the state of the person before us. Sometimes people call this "experiencing the soul of another." Again, this is not a mechanical process. We can merely ready ourselves by quieting down and being fully engaged. Whether we come to see with our sacred senses is a gift of God's grace.

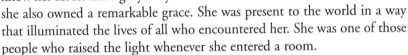

My mother-in-law, Marian Owens Lokvam, owned even more than what she could see. Those privileged to know her across her eighty-six years on this earth knew that she also owned a remarkable grace. She was present to the world in a way that illuminated the lives of all who encountered her. She was one of those people who raised the light whenever she entered a room.

To know presence, Marian didn't need to review a list of its key elements. She seemed to know these things intuitively. The rest of us, however, may benefit from remembering the three keys described here: Quieting, Full Engagement, and Spiritual Presence.

Like Elijah, God may come to us not in the storm and the fury, but in the silence of our hearts.

THE COMFORT
OF SILENT PRESENCE

To care means first of all to be present to each other.

—Henri Nouwen

A student of Dr. Nouwen's at Harvard Divinity School was walking with him across the campus after class. The student shared with Dr. Nouwen that his wife had recently passed away, at the age of thirty-two. Suddenly, the student found himself weeping uncontrollably.

What would the great Dr. Nouwen say? I wondered, as I listened to this story told to me by a psychologist at the Pastoral Counseling Centers of Tennessee. What words of wisdom would this great sage and author of over thirty books offer the grieving man in the middle of the Harvard campus?

If you have read Nouwen's work, you might guess the answer. Nouwen said nothing. Instead, after a while, he reached into his pocket, took out his handkerchief, and dabbed the man's tears.

Nouwen knew something many of us forget. The student's suffering was beyond words. But it was not beyond the comfort of a sweet gesture.

The great Parker Palmer reports a similar story. After he personally suffered through a terrible bout of depression, he wrote about the person who helped him more than anyone. It was a friend who stopped by his house every so often, sat across from him, and silently massaged his feet.

Many wonder what to *say* to someone whose son has been killed in an accident or whose daughter has been raped or whose mother has been murdered.

Nouwen and Palmer offer us wise counsel. Presence, particularly silent presence, may be the most welcome thing of all. Bringing food, massaging feet, dabbing tears, listening. These are valued gifts to a person seeking to purge grief.

Some of the frequently chosen alternatives to silence are troubling. We've all been present when some well-meaning soul tries to talk someone *out* of their suffering prematurely. "You'll be fine in a few days. This will pass," I heard someone say to the mother of an accident victim. They wanted her to "snap out of it," which, of course, would make it easier for them as well. It's hard to share suffering. Some wish the sufferer would just

cut out the crying and start smiling again. After all, wouldn't most of us prefer to skip the hard chapters of our life?

"Don't be sad," someone will instruct. "When God closes one window, he opens another." Maybe this is true for the speaker. But it may not feel comforting to the person who, at the moment, can only see darkness. The grieving person may even feel guilty: "Why can't I see the window yet?"

Another well-intentioned but misdirected choice is this commonly offered sentence: "I know *exactly* how you feel." None of us knows how the other person feels, even if we imagine we've had a similar experience. To tell someone we know their precise feelings is to devalue the unique and personal nature of the pain they are suffering.

It's odd how we sometimes forget common sense when seeking to offer comfort. If your son was killed in an accident, would you want someone to tell you, "Oh, you'll get over it"? That's not how grieving mothers and fathers feel. Instead, they feel broken and trapped in grief.

So why do we say such things? Perhaps we have temporarily misplaced our gift of empathy. Feeling uncomfortable for ourselves, we try to get the other person to stop crying—to stop making *us* uncomfortable. But it's about the other person, not us.

Of course, there are many good things we can say out loud. We can offer to keep the person in our thoughts and prayers, we can offer support, and we can remember to check in weeks later, after the early crowds have vanished. But this meditation is about illuminating the gift of silent presence.

My wife is a master at this. Fifteen years ago, when she learned of a friend's cancer diagnosis, she rose at five in the morning to deliver a basket of flowers and food to her friend's front door. She arrived before dawn in silence and left her gift in silence by the front door. Now, fifteen years into her recovery, my wife's friend still remembers this gesture as one of the most graceful and healing gifts—something that gave her hope to launch her journey back to health. It was beautiful, unexpected, and offered in silence.

We all need to grieve deep loss. People who try to nudge us through our grief prematurely may be innocently forcing a shortcut that harms the grief process. We must each work our own way along the path that leads out of suffering and grief. Yet how hopeful it is to know that caring friends are near along the way.

America's best caregivers, particularly those in hospice organizations like Alive Hospice in Nashville, often have an exquisite understanding of the power of offering silent presence to suffering. They know the words to offer and they also know that many times no words are adequate. They know that *staying present* with warmth and grace can be the most healing of all gifts. They appreciate that compassionate silence can offer a more powerful presence than the best-intentioned words.

QUESTIONS

■ Why is compassionate silence effective?

■ Why is it often difficult to be silent in the presence of grief?

■ What are some of the ways we demonstrate compassionate *being* as well as compassionate doing?

■ What are occasions when you have received kind gestures that meant a lot to you?

MINDFULNESS, MINDLESSNESS, AND GRACE

It has been my experience over and over again that there is hardly anything more difficult than to love someone.

—Rainier Maria Rilke

One of the greatest obstacles to being present is the human tendency to fall into the comfort zone of mindless repetition. Healthcare and charity work are flooded with tasks that, once done a few times, may rapidly become monotonous. How does the dishwasher on the other side of the cafeteria wall remain attentive to his or her work when they've done the same job eight hours a day for four years? How can the receptionist bring energy and light to each one of her hundreds of encounters each week? How does the nurse who has delivered a thousand babies bring his sense of joy and energy to delivery number one thousand and one?

As a child, I used to view some religious rituals as silly. What value could there be in repeating things just to repeat them? As I grew older, I learned about the challenge of mindfulness. A Catholic who recites the rosary mindlessly may yet gain some measure of peace. But compare this to the experience of the person of faith who repeats the rosary or other familiar prayers with an open heart and an attentive spirit.

The practice of mindfulness in meditation leads to mindfulness in caregiving. The practice of mindfulness to nature creates a greater ability for the soul to open to the pain of another. The practice of mindfulness to art, poetry, music, all enable us to see not only the beauty that is there, but to join with the agony that is always inherent in great beauty.

Truth is beauty. Truth is hard. Mindfulness to the most ordinary of our actions enriches not only our own life experience, but the lives of all those we encounter in our journey across our days and nights.

EXERCISE

Find a common object—perhaps the water bottle sitting on your desk. Observe it as if it were a thing of great beauty—for it may be. Tilt it. Watch

the way the water moves. Look past the nature of the substance we know as plastic and think of the way light travels through the ripples in the bottle, bounces off its facets, curls around its shape.

REFLECTION

Too often, people think beauty is reserved for red roses and purple sunsets. Beauty can exist in any place we look if we use our sacred eyes—in the withered skin of a dying patient, in the contorted face of an expectant mother in labor, in the eyes of an eight-year-old with cancer. The great (and unsung) caregivers on this earth are able to feel this kind of beauty and allow it to enrich their lives and the lives of those around them. These are individuals we think of as people of grace.

FINDING SILENCE WITHIN

Quiet without is helpful in finding silence within. External silence, however, is not always required for meditation. Some can meditate in the midst of noise—on planes, subways, even in the midst of football stadiums filled with screaming fans.

In my own meditations, I sometimes imagine myself *falling* into silence, sinking down, letting go of the energy that glued me to noise. Use these words if they help you find your place of peace.

Falling Silent

*Let yourself fall
towards silence.
The work will wait.
The people will live.
Life's traffic will swim
its strokes without you.
This is your time to rest
on the kind chest of silence.
Sit awhile in the quilted corner
of the one life that needs you.
The silence loves your
company.
Love her.
Breathe the song of your
sweet breath. Hear the air sway,
the hammock swing,
the sea's torso swell like yours
rises with the moon's tides.
Ride this current of quiet.
This is your time to rest.*

—E.C.

PROFOUND PRESENCE TO NOTHING IMPORTANT

Where attention goes, energy flows. If we offer intense presence to integrity and beauty, we will find love in that which has drawn the gift of our deep attention.

—E.C.

What commands your attention? Whatever it is, that's where the power of your energy is directed. Like millions of men and women, I've kicked an awful lot of Saturdays and Sundays through the goal posts directing my energy to men playing football. I enjoy watching sports, but part of me always wonders: So what?

Another thing I do in my idle time is water the grass. We have automatic sprinklers, but I also like to water the grass myself. As you know by now, most things are one kind of meditation or another to me and almost everything lends itself to allegory. Watering the grass has a function, of course. But I enjoy things like this more if I seek to appreciate the deeper meanings: the way sunlight catches the spray, the pressure of the hose against my hand, the smell of the wet grass.

So what? Football games, grass watering, driving to and from work. What draws attention during these in-between times in life? Meditation is about rest, relaxing and breathing while imagining images that support easing back from the noise of the world. There's no need to *do* anything other than gaze at streams of water as they strike the light.

Imagine yourself in a sunny day in the low seventies when the world is as gorgeous as it can become. Imagine the spray of water from a garden hose. Forget about the function of watering and shift attention to the water itself, to light, to color, to texture, to the fragrance of wet, to the feel of water and temperate air on the hands and in the face.

If the thing to which we give our attention has beauty, grace, elegance, integrity, we may come to love that thing. And the more we give to it or him or her our attention, the more we love— in part because of the investment of our hearts. After all, if we give years of our lives to caring for patients, we have invested enormous amounts of our energy.

Why invest energy in something we don't love? Why spend our days in work which is not our calling?

But what do we do when we become tired of something or someone we once thought we loved? Fatigue may develop because we have failed to see in a new way. Looking from another angle, we may discover, anew, a much richer dimension and texture to the the thing, the job, or the person we thought we knew. We may see life and brightness and golden light where we had come to see gray.

So this meditation is about more than sprays of water in a green-gold backyard in Tennessee. It is about *where* we put our attention and *how* we see. It is about looking in new and different ways at the common and the ordinary. It is about seeing the people we know at some level deeper than the thin slice of a single impression. It is about entering into communion with the other.

The essence of loving care is seeing the person for whom we care for as more than their surface, their so-called "vital signs." Yes, blood pressure and heart rate are important. *But the true vital signs are seen in the eyes, in the voice, in the touch.*

This is all about the phenomenon of what may be called *Profound Presence*. This is another phrase I use to describe sacred presence to the world around us. Profound Presence requires more than just looking carefully. The approach calls us to shake old patterns and common ways of seeing, to open the door to our souls as well as our hearts so that we may be present to the exquisite.

The world is flooded with the bright energy of love. It is available to us as a gift from God. What we are asked to do is to ease back from the day to day and to re-engage the world with sacred eyes. Caregivers know this in the intimacy of their experience with patients that, because of their pain, are deeply vulnerable.

Look again at the world you will encounter today. Love awaits us in the shadows as well as the sunlight. Drink the gift of this love. Know God's presence.

PRESENCE TO OUR WORK

Find a job you love and you'll never have to work a day in your life.

—Anonymous

On May 17, 2003, Pulitzer Prize–winning journalist Les Payne told University of Connecticut graduates, "There are too many professionals holding down well-paying jobs that they hate. Find a vocation that you can throw your life into." I wonder if they listened and today live his words. Most probably haven't and won't, wasting their talents in jobs they grow to hate.

For caregivers, work should be a calling, not just a job.

One of the reasons many don't live this wisdom is that we take our freedom to choose a job for granted and don't treat it as a gift to be respected. This is a gift many across the world wish they had.

The luxury of options is not available in many countries, including India, China, and sub-Saharan Africa, where many children are put to work at an early age and never know the choice of doing something they would like as adults. For them, life is a battle for daily survival just as it once was for American children.

Memorial Day and the 4th of July celebrate freedom and those who gave their lives so we would have choices in our democracy. Labor Day is an opportunity for caregivers to celebrate the choice we have to be present to our calling and to celebrate the career we have chosen.

It's good for us to remember those who lack such freedom. The theft of childhood by poverty and by oppressive employers is one of the things that led to the labor movement in America. In the 19th and early 20th century, children were put to work in grinding factory jobs and sent into dark coal mines where they were paid lower wages than adults simply because they were children. Women, as well, have been discriminated against in both hiring and wages. In general, many first-line employees have too often been subjected to oppressive work environments. Although the problem is less acute than it was previously, many employers manage to create unnecessarily difficult conditions for staff.

Today, most Americans can—with courage, persistence, and an open heart—choose to pursue their calling, especially if they are willing to make

mild compromises with the amount of money they make. Two questions present themselves: How do we find and pursue our calling, and how do we stay present to our work after we're accustomed to the routine of the job?

Here's a quick example of what it means to live your passion. It happens to be about my daughter. Two years into her practice of law, she realized she hated her work. In her late twenties, she recognized her true calling—to be a news photographer. Consider her obstacles to quitting law: 1) She would have to turn her back on seven years of advanced education, including four years at Harvard and a law degree from Tulane University, 2) she would have to put aside her two years of experience with a distinguished Boston law firm, and 3) she would have to take a 75% pay cut!

To her great credit, she found the courage to follow her passion. Now, more than five years into her new career, she's making less money and having much more fun. She faces each day with excitement and hope. A full-time photographer for the *Hartford* (Connecticut) *Courant*, she was recently selected as Photographer of the Year by the National Press Photographers Association for the entire New England area. And all of this is because she chose passion over paycheck.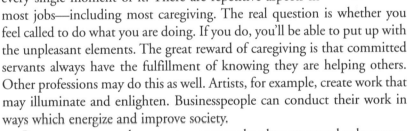

Loving your work, I might add, doesn't mean you love every single moment of it. There are repetitive aspects in most jobs—including most caregiving. The real question is whether you feel called to do what you are doing. If you do, you'll be able to put up with the unpleasant elements. The great reward of caregiving is that committed servants always have the fulfillment of knowing they are helping others. Other professions may do this as well. Artists, for example, create work that may illuminate and enlighten. Businesspeople can conduct their work in ways which energize and improve society.

Presence to our work means presence to the place we spend at least two-thirds of our waking lives.

If we've been in a job for a long time, it may be time for us to refresh and renew our vow to truly be present to the challenge before us. For caregivers, that challenge is in our hearts and it is in the eyes of the people around us—not only patients, but team members.

What's in it for you? Show up for work and you are showing up for your life.

THE SPEED OF THE SPIRIT

The heavenly spirit travels faster than the human eye can see, and slower than the human eye can see.

—anonymous quote passed on to me
by Claire Bateman

A friend, renowned poet Claire Bateman, sent me the above quotation after I complained to her that nobody ever remembers anything from sermons or speeches. "Maybe," she said, "but here's a line I've always remembered from a sermon I heard."

I can see why it stuck with her. The line calls us to a special kind of consciousness. We can't perceive the heavenly spirit with our human eyes, yet we can feel the presence of the heavenly spirit if we are open. What are ways we can become more fully present as the spirit travels through at speeds to fast and too slow to see?

An article on a lovely website called Spirituality and Practice (www.spiritualityandpractice.com), referred to me by a reader in California, says that "being present in the spiritual life always has a double meaning. There's present, as in here, in attendance. And there's present, as in now, a moment of time. What is the spiritual practice of being present? Being here now."

Where are we if we aren't fully here now? The answer is that we are reflecting on the past or daydreaming (or nightmaring) about the future. Whenever we are doing these things, we are robbing the present of our presence.

The way for us to return to the present is to engage in the regular practices we routinely recommend in the online *Journal of Sacred Work:* attending to breathing, noticing what is before us with our senses, and also learning how to see with sacred eyes. The human eye records what is before it. The human spirit feels and perceives what cannot be seen with the eye.

The reason spiritual practice encourages attending to the arts is that art appreciation requires that we slow down. A painting cannot be appreciated with a superficial glance, a poem cannot be absorbed without reflection, a piece of music cannot be engaged unless we are truly open to its tones, rhythms, and invisible communication with us.

Our days are flooded with velocity. If you live in a big or medium-sized city, you may believe you need to move fast to avoid being run down.

Speed can seem life-saving. Yet speed can kill as well. Spiritually, velocity can kill life's finest moments. Some people, women in particular, joke about this in the context of sexual experience. They tease about men being in a hurry. For either party to rush through an intimate encounter is to dishonor the sacredness of that experience and to miss the spiritual significance that rises from sharing love's secret.

The world will always be calling on us to move to the next thing. Yet the next thing will present itself whatever we do. Practicing presence means accepting that our senses are inadequate for the appreciation of the spiritual. That is why the human cannot see that which moves too fast *or* too slow for it. Only the spirit can see things the eye cannot. Only Love can open our spirits to the unique gift of her joy.

HEROES OF GRACE

When you're a healing presence, you're an artist.

—James E. Miller and Susan C. Cutshall,
The Art of Being a Healing Presence

She'll be ninety-four years old next month. She's far from being the oldest person in the country, but she's the most gracious one I know. You can see this grace in my mother's eyes—the sparkle and warmth that gracious people offer to us by their presence. Whatever I knew about grace as a child, I learned from her. From whom did *you* learn grace?

A new reader of our online *Journal of Sacred Work*, Tom Sheehan, sent me his nomination for the most compassionate person he knows:

"When she walks down the hall at the nursing home, balm, serenity, and comfort follow her as if an aura is loose on the premises. Beth Sheehan is the old-time nurse, talented, resourceful, responsive, and most of all, deeply compassionate. In her *whites* she is the personification of nursing, the most compassionate woman I have ever known."

Tom is writing about his wife. Across their decades of marriage, he has seen proof of his spouse's deep commitment to her work as a caregiver. "Who of us knows, in the tortured or confused mind of . . . patients, what touch is kindest or most temperate?" Tom asks. He thinks that Beth knows—and that she is the essence of love to her patients.

For some, the idea of healing presence is a mystery. Where does it come from? As Tom himself says in his letter: "I am never sure if it [compassion] carries her or she carries it, they are so intertwined, so interdependent."

Tracy Wimberly, R.N., is one of the most gracious people I've ever met. In a quarter-century of working together, as I watched her co-found Hospice at Riverside in Columbus and the Elizabeth Blackwell Center and head up Patient Care on my leadership team at Baptist Hospital System in Nashville, I often wondered about the source of her healing presence. Tracy grew up as the daughter of parents who were unable or unwilling to provide their presence to Tracy and her sister. So where did she learn her gift? She credits her grandmother. I credit Tracy. I believe she has spent her lifetime trying to develop the grace within her and to share it with others—to give others the love she may not have received in her growing-up years. Tracy's life is proof that each of us, with commitment, can enhance our gifts of our grace.

If healing presence is an art, as Miller and Cutshall offer in the quotation in this section, then caregivers may look to what artists do: they work on learning *how* to express their gift and they are constantly honing their *skills*. What else do they do? They study other great artists. Then they look within.

Healers need to do the same. We all have some gift of grace within us. We need to learn about how to express this gift, to practice it every day. And we can look to the models around us, the great heroes of grace that make us and others feel better whenever they enter our presence. Think of how Christians consider Jesus—one from whom some could gain healing merely by touching his clothes or hearing his voice.

Today I've introduced you to my own first model of grace—my mother. Perhaps these thoughts will re-introduce you to some of the people who have brought grace into your life. They have given you a gift. Pass it on.

EXERCISE

- Make a list of people you know who are your own heroes of grace. They may be famous people like Mother Teresa or Martin Luther King. Or they may be people you see at work every day.

- What are the characteristics of their presence that create this sense of grace?

- What do you see in their eyes, their tone of voice, their body language?

- Do they seem to be in a hurry?

- Going beyond their surface behaviors, what attitudes do you think lie beneath their behaviors? That is, how do you think they view others?

THE FLOWERS OF YOUR HUMANITY

We all have to find what best fosters the flowers of our humanity in this life and dedicate ourselves to that.

—Joseph Campbell

In 1970, I aimed a camera at a purple flower and snapped the shutter. I thought the photo was pretty good. It wasn't. The picture was as ordinary and plastic-looking as a fake smile.

Eleven years and thousands of photos later, I took the picture you see here. Across those years of looking, I came to see in a different way.

Find five minutes now. Better yet, find twenty. Within the quiet of closed eyes, can you see the flowers of your humanity blooming? Had you forgotten they were there? If you nurture these flowers every day, will it help them to grow so that they bloom without as well as within?

Find a quiet place within.
Close your eyes.
Let the world go.
Listen to the rhythm of
your breath.
In the dark of closed
eyes, watch
the flowers of your
humanity
bloom in your heart.
Rest.

OUR HIDDEN VOICE

So much of us remains hidden. So much of our voice, even when spoken, may never feel heard. To speak and not be heard is a painful life experience. It may cause us, in our fear, to lock away some of our best gifts in the darkest chambers of our hearts.

I feel a sadness for voices never heard, for gold lost in the shadows beneath the trees, for dear people I know who share just enough of their hearts to reveal that there is so much more living in the still waters of their souls.

Often

Often
I wonder about the stream
that flows beneath your voice,
the wordless current
that surges below syllables,
the hidden truth that courses
toward the unknown lake.

Often
I wonder what thoughts dwell
in the endless wells of your eyes.
What echoes sing to each other
in the caves that line the valley
or hide in the shadows away
from the sun-drenched flower?

Often
I imagine entering these waters
of yours, listening to your other
voices, hearing the music of your
secret songs.

—E.C.

SURRENDERING TO LOVE

Energy and will power are deeply important human strengths. Yet the three major monotheistic faiths, Judaism, Christianity, and Islam, preach surrender to God. This is the reason members of each faith bow to God in prayer, Moslems offering themselves prostrate five times a day. Surrender is difficult if we're confused about the meaning of God.

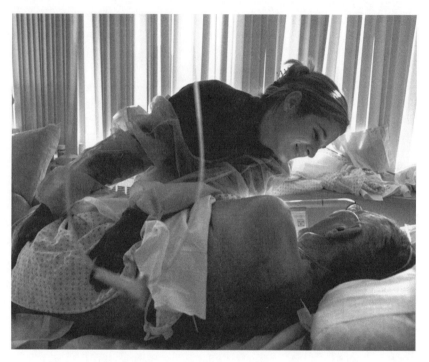

Difficulty arises if we choose to pit our will against God's Love. If you believe that God *is* Love, then, as a caregiver, you are joining Love's current as it flows through the world. My daughter, Tia, captured love in the face of a caregiver in this photo she took at Yale-New Haven Hospital on behalf of the *Hartford Courant* newspaper.

OUR SOUL AS HEALER

I f we think of our soul as the part of us most free of the the world's pull, perhaps our soul can be a source of healing. As we learn to become more in touch with our souls, we become more able to be present to others. Communing with the soul means leaving words behind. The journey may begin with words like the ones below. After the words, though, the soul speaks to us in other ways.

No Words

Tigers talk only with children.
What about souls?
    What if I asked you to listen to yours?
Would her whisper travel a pathway to your heart?

Would she sing spring gold, hum summer lavender,
celebrate autumn's tickertape parade,
chant plainsong to winter's still quilt?
I say the soul lacks seasons. I say she lives
evergreen in mountain air, muscled with light,
breathing soft beneath the ocean.
    I say she speaks without words,
        is heard without ears, and felt without hands.

    I say no scars mark her skin,
        for scars line hearts not souls.
I say the heart catches all arrows, bleeds, seeks soul's comfort.

The eyes of the soul hold holy light.
    Her hands know where to touch.
    Her ears hear the heart's moan.
    Her lips heal.
I say tigers talk, hearts bleed,
and only the soul knows the true and ancient music.
Rest in her arms.
Listen to her wordless song.
Let her hands heal.

                                    —E.C.

HOW WE MOVE

After young people go through our program, they move differently through the world.

—Village Cultural Arts Center

A group of African-American children, ages eight to fourteen, are gathered on a large blue mat in the center of a big room. Some sit in a circle, some sit in a row of chairs playing rhythmic instruments. In the center of the circle, two children face each other. They engage in a dance unusual to my eyes. They circle each other, sometimes jump over each other, rarely touch. "Respect the dignity of the circle," their leader, a man from South Africa, warns as one of the children acts restless. The child quiets down.

"Yes, we teach West African culture," the head of the Village Cultural Arts Center tells my colleague, Kristen Dinger, and me, "but we are really teaching pride, gratitude, respect, and positive approaches." That's when her partner chimed in with this memorable observation: "After young people go through our program, they *move differently* through the world."

How do we, as caregivers, move through the world? What kind of presence do we signal with the subtle movements of head, hands, the way we walk?

So much is signaled by body language. Social scientists claim that as much as ninety percent of communication happens not with words, but with the language of our movement—slight changes in facial expression, how we sit in a chair opposite someone, the raising or lowering of eyebrows, and whether we look the other person in the eye.

The people who are best at looking others in the eye are babies. A baby, lacking self-consciousness, can stare into your eyes for a long time. Many adults, of course, have great trouble with eye contact, especially if the other person is of the opposite sex.

Consider the difference between self-consciousness and self-awareness. Self-consciousness signals awkwardness and ego. Self-awareness suggests wisdom and grace. Similarly, "self-centered" connotes ego obsession. If we describe someone as "centered," however, this suggests we think of them as grounded and strong.

The children at the Village Cultural Arts Center are learning about being both self-aware and centered. In the course of discovering their roots, they are grounding themselves in ancient traditions that help them to value themselves. This strengthens their center. As a result, they make better life decisions.

Loving caregivers hold in their hands a golden thread that represents a long and hallowed tradition that mixes compassion with skill. Loving care does not involve compassion alone. Caregivers train themselves to deliver the gifts of both competency and emotional presence. It takes discipline, self-awareness, and centering to become a great caregiver. Just like the growing of a beautiful garden, it takes daily nurturing to enhance our mindfulness so that we may be loving servants to others.

REFLECTION

How do you move through this world? Does the way you carry yourself signal warmth, openness, and competence all at the same time? Our actions are, of course, informed by our thoughts. *Those who cultivate love move through the world differently than those who live out of fear.*

After I meditate, I know that I move through the world differently than I did before I took that twenty-minute break. I know that I am able to listen better, to concentrate better, to be more present to the world and more centered. This is partly because prayer and meditation dissolves some of the distracting noise in the world and enhances my ability to focus on what matters.

MEDITATION

Take five minutes (or twenty) now, close your eyes, feel the rhythm of your breath.

HOW LOVE MOVES THROUGH US

L'amor che move il sol e l'altre stelle

—last line of Dante's *Divine Comedy*

My Italian son-in-law tells me that the last line of Dante's masterwork means (translated from the archaic Italian) "the love that moves the sun and the other stars." In the Comedy, the people come outside to be in the presence of this magnificent force—the Love of God.

The greatest gift of our human existence is the chance we have to witness God's grace and power. This love that moves the sun and all the other stars can guide the hands and eyes of caregivers as well. You carry this gift with you and unwrap it for others when you reach out from your heart to help another.

So many turn their backs on love. So many, blinded by the repetitive nature of certain tasks or scarred by previous rejections, lose their chance to bring the presence of God to their sacred encounters with the sick and vulnerable.

In today's meditation, we have the chance to pause, to breathe, and to contemplate the many chances we will have on this day to let love pass through us and into the lives of others.

Each caregiver has the chance to affect the lives of so many. Our kind acts awaken the energy of love in ways that ripple out beyond our knowing. Your kindness to one breeds his or her kindness to another in ever-widening circles. This multiplier effect means that each compassionate action plants the seeds for love to flower in many places.

MEDITATION

Today is the only day you have and now is your only chance to let Love stream through you into the eyes and hearts and souls of strangers.

Today, as the stars hide above the shrouded sun and beaded curtains of rain sweep the high mountains clean and a

solitary swallow arrows over the tiled roof of an old Spanish Mission, you remember your mission. Where is your heart today? Will you unwrap its gifts? Will the love that moves the sun and the other stars move through you before today's light leaves the sky?

REFLECTIVE PRACTICE

Consider a daily practice that will help to remind you to engage your gift of love. This could be something as simple (but powerful) as pausing for three seconds at a patient's door before you enter. This is a chance for you to repeat a reminder to yourself. This patient is special and so are you. How can you combine your special gifts with the needs of the person before you? Imagine the power of this—a three-second pause—long enough for you to catch your breath and remember your gift of loving care.

WHEREVER YOU ARE

We may occupy more locations than the place in which we breathe at this moment. We live in the minds of those who think of us and care for us. And some part of us lives in the places we have been and might be in the future. Wherever you are, you, as a caregiver, have the chance to live not in your yesterday or your tomorrow, but in your now.

Caregivers are the subjects of great demands because they are presented with such great needs from others. We place a heavy burden on caregivers to ease our pain, cure our disease, sit with us in the midst of our anger and sadness as well as in our happiness and joy. The challenge to conscientious caregivers is not how to *take* a break, but how to *give* themselves a break.

Poets always say it better. And Mary Oliver says it best of all in these words.

Wild Geese

You do not have to be good.
You do not have to walk on your knees
for a hundred miles through the desert, repenting.
You only have to let the soft animal of your body
love what it loves.
Tell me about despair, yours, and I will tell you mine.
Meanwhile the world goes on.
Meanwhile the sun and the clear pebbles of the rain
are moving across the landscapes,
over the prairies and the deep trees,
the mountains and the rivers.
Meanwhile the wild geese, high in the clean blue air,
are heading home again.
Whoever you are, no matter how lonely,
the world offers itself to your imagination,
calls to you like the wild geese, harsh and exciting—
over and over announcing your place
in the family of things.

—Mary Oliver

PEACE

Peace, like happiness, eludes pursuit. Instead, perhaps we can cultivate her presence, invite her into our lives, establish the kind of garden in our hearts where peace feels welcome and can bloom anew.

—E.C.

My friend and colleague Tracy Wimberly, R.N., and I worked together in all three hospital systems where I was privileged to serve as CEO. Her favorite greeting has always been, "Peace." She used to have a china plaque on her office door bearing the same word in green letters.

Peace. The word has a lovely energy around it for most people. Just the saying of it or the reading of this single word imparts to some a feeling of rest. The great Peter Paul Rubens even sought to paint Peace.

One of the goals of our online *Journal of Sacred Work* is that it be a place of *sanctuary* for caregivers. A place where caregivers and all other caring people can come for rest.

Because there is very little we can do to calm the big troubles of this world, the best kind of peace may be found within, not from without. We share poetry and images in the hope that some combinations of words and pictures will help to awaken the energy of peace within the reader.

I found a poem by Kenneth Rexroth from his book *The Lights in the Sky Are Stars*. I hope it might bring you, in its imagery, some moments of peace.

The Heart of Herakles

Lying under the stars
In the summer night,
late, while the autumn
Constellations climb the sky,
As the Cluster of Hercules
Falls down the west
I put the telescope by
And watch Deneb
Move towards the zenith.
My body is asleep. Only

My eyes and brain are awake.
The stars stand around me
Like gold eyes. I can no longer
Tell where I begin and leave off.
The faint breeze in the dark pines,
And the invisible grass,
The tipping earth, the swarming stars
Have an eye that sees itself.

—Kenneth Rexroth

Peace, like happiness, eludes pursuit. Instead, perhaps we can cultivate her presence, invite her into our lives, establish the kind of garden in our hearts where peace will bloom. This means that when we are confronted with peace's opposite—violence—we respond with love and kindness.

I read recently that justice begins with compassion, not with anger. This is the peace which Jesus held when he was confronted by crowds shouting at him, spitting at him, and reviling him.

It is also the peace cultivated by the Amish. In their response to the family of the hate-filled man in Pennsylvania who molested and killed some Amish children, the Amish offered love and forgiveness. And it is seen in that powerful scene in the film "To Kill a Mockingbird" when an enemy approaches Atticus Finch (played brilliantly by Gregory Peck) and spits in his face. Peck, looking a foot taller than his antagonist, simply reaches in his back pocket, pulls out his handkerchief, wipes his face, and walks away.

Do we have that kind of strength to live peace when confronted by a rude and angry patient or family member? Perhaps we may cultivate inner peace so powerfully that we will find love's strength in future confrontations with those who have lost this gift.

Herakles was a son of Zeus. He was considered, in Greek mythology, half man and half God, and was both loved and hated by the Immortals in whom the ancient Greeks believed. The Cluster of Herakles is a grouping of stars. It is also referred to as the constellation Hercules, one of the largest in the universe.

HOW ART TEACHES LOVING CARE

What else can one do, when we think of all the things we do not know the reason for, than go look at a field of wheat?

—Vincent Van Gogh, in a letter to his sister
one month before his death, 1890

During the summer of 1890, Van Gogh, in love with beauty, spent lots of time studying a field of wheat near Auvre-sur-Oise, France. He painted for us what he saw in an immortal image titled *Wheatfields with Reaper*, now owned by the Toledo Museum of Art. It was one of his last works. What can Van Gogh teach us about loving care?

"I myself am quite absorbed," he wrote to his sister, "in the immense plain with wheat fields against the hills, boundless as a sea, delicate yellow, delicate soft green, the delicate violet of a dug-up and weeded piece of soil, checkered at regular intervals with the green of flowering potato plants, everything under a sky of delicate blue, white pink, violet tones."

A Chicago Art Institute study that revealed that most visitors spend only seven seconds looking at masterpieces also indicated something else: The reason those visitors were only spending that seven seconds was because they were doing *informational looking*. Once they figured out what the painting was supposed to depict and made a brief assessment of whether they liked it, they moved on.

Wiser viewers (including a group of experts studied separately) spent much longer with a given painting, sometimes studying it for over an hour and coming back the next day and the next day to look again and again. These wiser viewers understand that great visual art is like a Shakespearean play—it can be seen again and again and each time the experience can become richer.

Many caregivers make the seven-second mistake with patients. They walk in the room, take a quick look at the patient, do a rapid physical assessment, and move on. In so doing, they miss the chance for a more meaningful encounter—the kind of encounter that can enrich their work as well as the life of the patient.

One requirement for great art appreciation and great caregiving is that we slow down, listen for love speaking through the artist and through us, watch for what the artist has tried to say to our hearts through our eyes. Then we need to transfer that understanding to our caregiving. For loving care requires that we slow down, listen for love, let her light shine through us to help heal the need of another.

Artists, like caregivers, often suffer as they struggle up the Mount Everest of their souls. They give all of themselves to their creations. Can we find as much courage in *appreciating* what they have done for us? Can we give of ourselves to others?

What is the communion between a caregiver and a person in need (whether that person is a patient, a fellow caregiver, or a family member)? Loving caregiving is an art. *Great caregivers are great artists.* The fact that their work is usually done anonymously does not detract from the genius of their accomplishments. Indeed, Van Gogh was ignored across his career and created his masterpieces in near anonymity, selling only one of his creations during his lifetime.

America's finest caregivers act anonymously as well. They are, as Mother Teresa said, doing "small things with great love."

If you seek to become a great caregiver, enter into communion with artists. It can be tough work, like caregiving itself.

Work past your uncertainty about poetry and painting and listen for how the artist can inform your heart. Spend real time before exceptional art. Listen to world-class music like Mozart and Beethoven and Bach again and again. Spend time with poetry by contemporary geniuses like Maya Angelou and Billy Collins. The gifts of beauty are there if we can slow down, learn, listen, and find the persistence to stay with the artist's gift until we have unwrapped it. From the passion of great artists, we can learn great caregiving. Because art and caregiving are about the same thing—passionate commitment.

As you receive these exquisite gifts of art, you will be better able to give the beautiful gift of your special presence to the people who need your help. Let the genius of great art inform your life as you learn to live the love of true caregiving.

INVITATION

Find a great work of art on the Internet or elsewhere. Study it for five minutes. Read about it. Come back later and look at it again. After the first

seven seconds, you will have one impression. Longer looks will cause you to see more and more as your mind moves past informational looking to the real experience of seeing with your heart.

Spend some real time with someone in need. If you stay awake to the encounter, you will begin to see deeper beyond the surface of the person before you to discover the richer layers within.

MOTHERING AND CAREGIVING

For most of the world's population, our very first experience of love is through our mothers. It is mother who is the first to coo love to us, to hold us to her breast, to wrap us in her warmth. Regardless of our age, it is mother we most often call for when we are frightened or in pain. As babies, and beyond, we seek a mother's love.

Some psychologists posit that people who have trouble with caregiving may not have received this loving warmth as babies and small infants. Clearly there are exceptions, surrogates who stepped in to give love when a mother died in childbirth or was, for whatever other reason, unable to offer the gift of love to her baby. Our mothers (or their stand-ins) are the ones who teach us love before we can speak.

Recall the person who first gave you love. Consider how you are passing that gift to others in your work. Read Ancle Rubin's lovely reflection on motherhood from "Sitting in the Grass," brought to my attention by reader Emily Fluhrer of Greenville, South Carolina.

> *Sitting in the grass*
> *under the stars*
> *by the extinguished fire.*
> *sitting there after the last trip*
> *with a jug and a pail of water.*
> *amazed at how long the wet logs*
> *continue to sizzle.*
> *mistaking a firefly in the grass*
> *for a spark,*
> *confusing, as I look up,*
> *stars and fireflies,*
> *thinking, though, about my mother.*
> *looking at the brilliant pricks of light*
> *in the dark sky,*
> *at the dark shapes of trees,*
> *darker than the sky they stand up against,*
> *thinking about how much I love*
> *what is no longer visible.*

telling my mother out loud,
not loud, really, but very quietly
saying her name
the personal name I had for her
speaking it to the night sky
as our ancestors would
pray to those
who went before
and lit a path back
to the source.

—Ancle Rubin, "Sitting in the Grass"

MEMORY OF LIFE: THE NEED FOR RESPITE

Billy Collins, America's former Poet Laureate, offers us poetry that is not only brilliant but accessible. As caregivers consider how poetry can enrich their lives, they may look to this example of his poignant insight and consider how poetry can enrich and inform the lives of caregivers who, in this case, may be looking after those who have forgotten key things in their lives—the names of their children, their own name, what happened five minutes ago.

Collins's poetry surprises many who have feared language written in stanzas. As they read his words, they are pleased to discover a new presence to life.

Forgetfulness

The name of the author is the first to go
followed obediently by the title, the plot,
the heartbreaking conclusion, the entire novel
which suddenly becomes one you have never read,
never even heard of,

as if, one by one, the memories you used to harbor
decided to retire to the southern hemisphere of the brain,
to a little fishing village where there are no phones

Long ago you kissed the names of the nine Muses goodbye
and watched the quadratic equation pack its bag,
and even now as you memorize the order of the planets,

something else is slipping away, a state flower perhaps,
the address of an uncle, the capital of Paraguay.

Whatever it is you are struggling to remember,
it is not poised on the tip of your tongue,
not even lurking in some obscure corner of your spleen.

It has floated away down a dark mythological river
whose name begins with an L as far as you can recall,
well on your own way to oblivion where you will join those
who have even forgotten how to swim and how to ride a bicycle.

No wonder you rise in the middle of the night
to look up the date of a famous battle in a book on war.
No wonder the moon in the window seems to have drifted
out of a love poem that you used to know by heart.

Collins's charming and heartbreaking poem touches the way we perceive life. Our memory informs so much of our being that we can't imagine being without it, much less gradually beginning to lose it.

Caregivers who look after Alzheimer's patients encounter, every day, the strange images of perfectly normal-looking human beings who can't recall what happened five minutes ago. If you've been close to someone who has experienced this hard reality, you have a feeling for the challenge caregivers face.

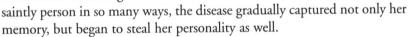

Years ago, my late mother-in-law, who had looked after her stroke-ridden husband faithfully for many years, traveled the tortuous descent into the painful valley of Alzheimer's. A lifelong lover of literature and drama, and a saintly person in so many ways, the disease gradually captured not only her memory, but began to steal her personality as well.

The process can leave us wondering who we are.

Landmark studies by Drs. Ronald and Jan Glaser at Ohio State University have demonstrated the enormous stress caregivers face, especially family members who may be engaged in round-the-clock care. The Glasers have demonstrated that stressed caregivers suffer from increased physical illness and that they recover more slowly from injuries.

A small number of high-quality respite programs around the country recognize and treat this problem by offering relief to caregivers. In light of the rising population of the elderly, our country needs to recognize the dramatic need for respite care and the need for significant funding of these programs.

Meanwhile, if you know a caregiver who's taken the responsibility to look after a patient with dementia, or anyone else who's housebound, today is an opportunity to begin offering help, and the respite our love can bring, before we become the ones who "forget."

HUMAN CLOSENESS

In human closeness there is a secret edge . . .

—Anna Akhmatova (1889–1966)

The complex caregiver/patient encounter has so many facets. The more acute the patient's need, the greater the opportunity for the encounter to be meaningful.

Opening our hearts in patient and client encounters means that the caregiver will feel some of the pain of the patient. There is a cost in this. But there is also a cost if we close the door to our soul.

The right emotional distance for caregivers is a continuing challenge to those who remain awake and sensitive to their calling. The "secret edge" of closeness can feel dangerous. Yet, as Henri Nouwen has written so eloquently, "Those who do not run away from our pains but touch them with compassion bring healing and new strength."

When caregivers retreat from a heartful openness to those in need they exchange one kind of pain for another. They may save themselves from tears, but they risk becoming unfeeling automatons.

Still, the natural inclination of so many caregivers is to run for the hills when, for example, a patient dies. "Don't get too close to your patients," some hardened veteran will warn.

Is it possible to get too close? Of course. But the greater risk is distance. Clinical distance, a phrase often used in professional training, is often mistakenly interpreted by caregivers as a kind of cold detachment, an arrogance that casts the caregiver as a powerful monarch ruling the fate of the patient.

This is the syndrome that can birth the so-called "God complex" in which caregivers, particularly doctors, accept a sort of deification from those who seem to idolize their performances—as if it were the doctor's skill alone that was responsible for a patient's recovery.

Humility calls caregivers to appreciate that every successful healing experience and every sacred encounter is a partnership of many people and many forces. That the key to great caregiving is the practice of Radical Loving Care.

May we all extend our deepest admiration to the men and women who find the courage and strength each day to share the pain of the people they treat.

The Burning House

Wanting to alleviate pain without sharing it is like wanting to save a child from a burning house without the risk of being hurt.

—Henri Nouwen

Without warning,
they die, abandoning you as if to insult your
skill, your commitment, your caring
and everything you did to heal. As if to mock how close

you came to their heart. They
left you feeling that you could
be their bridge to life, their hope, their salvation
and you arrive at work to hear, "She died this

morning at 5:04 a.m." You know that you were
sleeping
then, dreaming that your heroic efforts would extend
the thread of her time, and she, to whom you gave
your
heart, is gone.

How hard to love, to give, to live knowing that
your heart must give and bear this burning blow,
this crimson slashing, this secret edge.
Will there be healing,
new strength?

—E.C.

INVITATION TO SANCTUARY

In 1888 a children's book, *The Secret Garden* by Frances Hodgson Burnett, appeared in bookstores across England. Its enduring popularity led to two film versions (1949 and 1993).

Why is the story so popular? Perhaps we all imagine a place as magical as the one in the story—a garden paradise hidden behind high walls where spring blooms eternal. In the story, the garden proves to be a healing presence for the main character (as well as others). This is the image I offer to you today. Your own secret garden. Each of us can create a place like that within us. A place we can visit behind closed eyes as we take some minutes to rest and restore ourselves.

> *You who are covered in tasks. You who are*
> *busy with the needs of others. You who need*
> *to give yourself rest's gift. Come with me up*
> *the path. I invite you to sit awhile, to nurture*

> *your tired parts so that, refreshed, you may rise again. Stay.*
> *Breathe deeply the air of God's love, exhale fatigue. Breathe*
> *in the hope of this day, exhale the sharp fragments of anger*
> *and frustration. Breathe in the fresh air of justice and tolerance,*

> *exhale the poison of bias and judgment. This*
> *is your time of rest. The bench in my*
> *backyard awaits you. The willow oak above*
> *it will shelter you, evergreens will shield*

> *your privacy, hydrangea will flower your eyes. Remove your*
> *shoes. Toe the grass. Come. Sit. Rest for every second of the*
> *five minutes you take today. These sanctuaries live within.*
> *Let them encircle you in silence. Breathe faith, breathe*

> *hope, breathe love. For you are a child of God. Your heart*
> *is a garden of love. Your angels hover near wondering if you'll*
> *notice their presence. The water in the fountain is alive with*
> *light and song. The shadows beneath each leaf are*
>   *hiding places.*

Behind closed eyes, there is only your world.
Let the breeze of angels' wings brush your neck.
In the cake that is this day, carve a five-minute
slice of your own. Take. Eat. Breathe love.

Find rest in the
secret garden of your heart
where the living water flows.

—E.C.

THE WAITING ROOM

Today, millions of people will go to hospitals, clinics, and doctor's offices for care. Instead of being seen right away, they will be assigned to a particular part of the world called The Waiting Room.

I wish the nurse would call me like my mother
did long ago.
 "Come, here, son." and I would
go to her and she would wrap me in her
  warmth.
I wish the nurse would call my name
  as if glad to see me.
I wish she would hear my fear, know
that I am human,
  even some mother's
son.

—E.C.

PASSING ACQUAINTANCES

Presence to the ordinary helps us see the extraordinary.

—E.C.

I nside any given day we have countless tiny encounters that are random and forgettable. How can these brief glimpses inform the texture of deeper, more meaningful meetings?

At dawn, we awaken to some kind of light, we brush aside the covers, our feet touch the floor. The news comes to us that it's Monday. We are seconds into our waking and there is nothing, yet, to mark the day as anything other than ordinary.

In first light, we glance out the window as a light breeze scuttles a leaf across the driveway. We see nothing special and the leaf leaves our life, never to be thought of again or spoken about. On the way to work, we see a woman at a bus stop in a worn purple coat. She smiles gap-toothed at someone. But we are already past her and she exits our lives. Driving by a self-storage company whose outer wall is painted with a long wavy blue line like the surface of the ocean, we see a man in a corduroy coat walking the sidewalk as if immersed in those waves. He, too, will join the endless list of those we forget, bit characters in the drama of our lives. But there are those we encounter in ways so meaningful to us that we remember special things about many meetings. They are the ones with whom we have shared such a profound presence that they live integrated into our hearts.

There are strangers we brush past and people who live so close to our hearts we feel they are a part of us. In-between, we caregivers may find some understanding of what it means to be present to someone who may need our gifts for only a brief season of their suffering.

I thought of all of these—the dying leaf, the woman in purple, the man in corduroy, people I love, and those I have yet to meet—after rising one Monday morning and driving to work along the route I take every day.

Autumn Acquaintances

I will not speak of you again,
your brittle back
curling so that your leaf tips fingernail the brick

of my backyard. You scramble-scuttle
on your calloused toes, shooed by gusts
past the frozen tree that was your mother,
running from me forever. I will not speak of you again.

Nor will I speak of you again, you that are benched
at the bus stop bunched in your purple winter coat,
tonguing your divided teeth.

Perhaps the ancient blood of Bantu kin
threads the rivers beneath your skin.
I want to grant you an honored place
on the tiny stage of these lines,
for you look old—poor and deserve,

       at least, this recognition before your exile to,
       I hope, Shangri-la.

Nor will I speak again of you, my corduroy-
coated man, as you parallel the waves
undulating the long wall of the Abbott
Self-Storage Company on your way to somewhere
far beyond the brittle leaf in my yard; or of the cars
blurring or the voices singing on the wire strings
that sag post to post to wooden post.

And who would speak,
even once, of that fire hydrant's stubbed arms?

But you I will speak of again, for I remember when
the sun caught the left edge
of your suddenly chatoyant eyes
as you curled cat-like,
sun slanting so that I needed to stroke
the landscape of your soft back,
ease your loneliness, and think of you
again, again, again.

                         —E.C.

PHOTO MEDITATION

To look at something is such a wonderful thing of which we still know so little. When we look at something, we are turned completely toward the outside by this activity. But just when we are most turned toward the outside...things seem to take place within us that have longed for an unobserved moment...

—Rainer Maria Rilke

Take a look at this photograph of silk and lace and sensual elegance. Spend a full minute or more contemplating it. If this image is restful for you, carry it in your heart across this week. Perhaps it will soften the hard edges of your days.

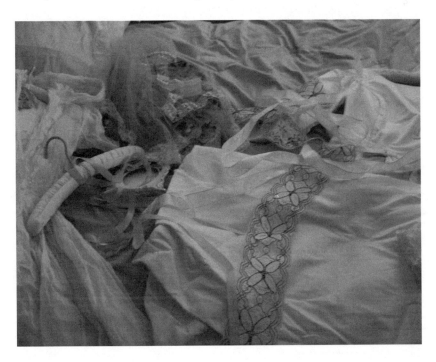

TODAY

Spread out on grains of sand
in Northern Kenya
mothers hold children who
will die today of starvation
and there is nothing we can do
about that, we say,
for anyone so far away
except to pray.

Killing bands burst from
jungle hiding places
to machete Muslims/Christians
in Nigeria today
and there is nothing we can do,
we say,
for anyone so far away
except to pray.

In the mountains of northern
Pakistan
it's so cold today that, here in the dawn
of the twenty-first century
children will freeze to death.
and there is nothing we can do,
we say
for anyone so far away
except to pray.

Within our sight
within our touch
souls cry for help right here,
not far away.
Will we do more than pray
What? How much?
*   and will it be today?*

—E.C.

A MOUNTAIN LAKE EXPERIENCE

Consider the difficulty of really looking at a painting. The forces of the world—schedules, agendas, lists—yank us from our center and toss us about so that we may feel like flotsam riding ocean cross-currents. Radios play, televisions sell their messages, e-mail asks for answers, cell phones shout, videogames dance. Each calls like a siren for our attention. Your own thoughts may shout louder than all the other noise so that you are frightened to take the minutes of silent meditation your soul needs to help you thrive in this world.

What kinds of noise circle about you now? How is your attention, your presence to the deepest needs of others, your ability to hear the music of your own soul?

Caught in the swirl, it is no wonder that America's caregivers, beeped at, paged, blinked at by call lights, may lose touch with the core of their calling—to care for those in need, to offer healing, to be present to pain and joy—to be present to real light instead of its electric imitations.

Competing demands dilute our ability to heal with love. They interfere with our capacity to appreciate the beauty around us and to live our love.

Early caregivers understood the power of presence—the need to be heard and to be loved. Those who cultivate presence in long interactions are also more effective at being present in brief encounters. The practice of meditation is the exercise most likely to further our ability to be present to others. It is a gift we give ourselves and, in turn, becomes a gift we give to others.

PRESENCE MEDITATION

Take a full minute with the lovely work The Lake of Zug, 1843, a painting by the mid-nineteenth century artist William Turner. You can see it on the Internet by entering in Google the phrase: "William Turner, Lake of Zug."

POETRY MEDITATION

You may wish to write a poem based on your meditation on a beautiful painting. I wrote this one after looking at Turner's Lake of Zug for a minute that was full and rich and peaceful for me.

Turner's Lake

Outside me, three tree branches dance above bunches
of nervous cars driven by blank-faces waiting for
red to go green, tires to turn, the radio to play the next song.

Back within, I sit, close my eyes, open my heart's door. It's time
to visit an Alpine lake the way Turner watercolored one in
1843's summer. The elbow of the steep blue mountain blocks
the sun's effort to define itself. What light there is hazes the
lake below.

In the left distance, two men boat. In the right foreground,
children rock-scramble. In the lower left, two-inch-high
women thigh-deep the lake, wash clothes they aren't
wearing, air their skin near brown rocks and blue
water. Near the dying man

I will care for today, others edge to the end of their
earthly visit. Today, I will take my patient's hand, lis-
ten to his pictures. When he falls asleep,

I will stay awhile, pour out a blue lake, arrange some
rocks around it. Nearby, mountain peaks will pierce the sky,
children play, women wash clothes and two men will sway in
a wooden boat that will never reach the shore.

—E.C.

A Gift for You

What do you see in the painting now? How do you feel? Pick a painting or photograph of your own choice and give it to yourself as a gift to guide a personal meditation. Spend time with it—one minute, five minutes, twenty minutes. Then put it in one of your heart's pockets and carry it with you across the day. This gift will become a present for all those around you.

REST IN THE ORDINARY

As you may know, Geishas spend years learning how to prepare and pour a cup of tea with complete grace. The tea ceremony becomes a meditation.

We who have been raised in the west may never have imagined how ordinary work can become a meditation. In 1978, I took this photograph of a woman sweeping steps near a sidewalk in Montreal. This photograph hangs in our home. Whether this woman imagines her sweeping as a meditation or not, her image has become a meditation for me—a reminder of how the heart may rest while the hands work.

CARING FOR ANGRY CAREGIVERS

Surgeons, as well as other caregivers, work day and night near the scalpel-edge of life and death. When a patient dies, feelings of anger and guilt may descend on these caregivers. How can we help healers heal when their hearts have been broken? The temptation for many is to try to "fix" the grief and anger. Yet healing requires that we first be present to the caregiver's pain. I imagined this prose poem based on thirty years of listening to physicians and other caregivers share the pain, anger, and grief they feel when a patient they thought would survive, suddenly dies.

A Surgeon's Anger

The mouth of the garage swallows me . . .

and I remember I don't remember the drive home from the hospital along a path I've beaten senseless in twenty years of travel.

Shards of anger penetrate, aggravate, prickle the way fiberglass tortures skin if touched bare-handed.

I must hide in the garage, let time transform me to the husband/father who loves wife/children sitting innocent in the home I bought for their comfort/mine and I'm bleeding-breathing/crying anger-knotted—as if the embolus that killed my patient stole my breath as well.

I bleed for the family behind me that I couldn't comfort, for the crying friend I hurried by pretending to rush to another surgery (my face masked like a thief). But I had no more cases and I know my last patient no longer needs me. Dead men need no doctors and I boil with grief, bereft at how this man I cared for left this world.

The indifferent garage hears the heated engine tick-snap. Tears cool slow as rain. I repeat: "My patient no longer needs me. My patient no longer needs me. My patient no longer has any needs. . . ."

I let go of the steering wheel. To let. To let go and oh . . . Why pour my anger on others? I reason, as I feel another scar form on my soul's skin.

Inside, wife wants husband, children need father. Inside, I need the patience God has. Inside, I need the God my patient has.

Doctors, nurses—anyone close to saving life—know the risks involved in their work. Meditations, to be meaningful, need to recognize the brutal edges of life as well as her soft curves and sunny meadows. When their hearts are open, caregivers may feel not only heartache but, often, a sense of guilt after the death of a patient. These painful feelings may cause hearts to close and the delicate balance of compassion and competence to be lost.

The Baptist Healing Trust, under the guidance of Keith Hagan, M.D. and with the help of Drs. Roy Elam, Cheryl Fassler, and Liz Krueger, has formed an initiative called Caring for the Caregiver. In this work, physicians meet to share the experience of their practice in the hope that this sharing will, in and of itself, bring balance and healing. Their work rests in part on the wise teaching of Rachel Remen, M.D. For more information, contact us.

PRESENCE TO GRIEF

You lower your head,
stare at your hands,
wait for me as if I held a magic wand
that would dissolve the gray cloud

hovering too near. But I don't
wave a wand or say
anything
as the anonymous traffic rumbles by

along the busy street on the other side
of the wall. The ceiling
light fingers your hair, descends
the angles of your face, is trapped
in the ellipses that rain from your
heart.

I don't say anything and you don't say
anything. The cloud turns, wanders
toward the horizon the way a gunslinger
abandons his victim in the center of the street.

You raise your head, shake your hair,
sigh-smile.

I hear a little girl gasping for air
after holding her breath for too long
inside the dark body
of a lake,

how grateful she is
to breathe again.

—E.C.

BE

What does it mean to be?
Be the kind hand that reaches out
to calm someone's need.
Be the heart that opens
in spite of its own pain.
Be the arm that circles to salve
another's pain, strong as
an oak limb, gentle as its leaves.
Awaken the best angels within you.
Christen your life with meaning.
Join the servants of light.
Be a lover.

—E.C.

THE POETRY OF AFFECTION

Too many people fear poetry and, in the process, rob themselves of the joy that comes from letting a special wave of love flow through their hearts. The poem in this meditation is not presented for its high excellence, but for its way of expressing affection—in this case, from husband to wife.

When is the last time you assembled words of affection and shaped them into an arrow aimed toward someone you love? Tonight, write love to someone, whether you find the courage to send it or not. It doesn't have to be perfect—simply motivated by affection.

Imagine the impact your love can have on another. David Whyte has said about poetry: "Work is a very serious matter indeed. We freight our work with meaning and identity, and fight hard and long for some kind of purpose in our endeavors. Organizations need to understand the wellsprings of human creativity in order to shape conversations that are invitational to an individual's greater powers. Good poetry can provide explosive insight, grant needed courage and stir the dormant imagination of individuals and organizations alike."

Here is a poem I wrote recently for my wife.

Conference in the Clouds

When the gods gathered that spring for their regular
conference in the clouds, I wonder if some beams
of sunlight shaped themselves into twin arrows
pointing them towards you and me. What

winds hummed through their airy hands,
tuned their heavenly ears to the harmony
of our hearts, our need for each other?
What comments from their research angels

advised them of the special fit of you to me? Or
did they meet at midnight in moonlight, sew epaulets
of stars on their shoulders, laugh all night? Was it
the warm drafts of that eve that ordained them with

*the wisdom to know that you and I must be combined
so they could rest easy, rise with us at dawn, smile over
their morning coffee at their genius in creating such an
alchemy of passion, anger, foolishness, joy, love?*

—E.C.

REFLECTION IN VERSE

All experience is an arch wherethrough gleams that untravelled world whose margin fades for ever and forever as I move.

—Alfred Lord Tennyson

The black-and-white child digs a hole in the sand,
an opening to a world that is long gone.
The camera didn't preserve
the colors of the day. Those left
along with the child who
dug the hole, along with the small hands
that held the shovel, along with
the young mother and younger sisters,
along with that day's sun and wind,
along with the umbrellas that have long
since been folded, tossed, replaced,
along with the waves that swept that
shore on that day. All of that is gone, and
all of that is still here,
informing this moment,
gleaming through the arch
of 1949 and into this day.

—E.C.

THE WELL OF MEMORY

Within us flows an artesian well of memories. The mind can dip into the well of memory, allowing us to drink from the past—the bitter and the sweet.
This well holds so much of our life. Drink from it today.

1952

It's there, isn't it, that ancient leaf
baking in the hard sun on a griddle
of earth?

It's there, isn't it, that Sierra stream
that wets all those throatless stones.

You alone can drink from
her in an afternoon old as a
a mountain peak, new as now.

The wind rises, pine needles
whisper their gossip and it's

there, isn't it? Beneath the intimacy
of eyes, tucked between heartbeats,
folded in thoughtskin, lodged below
a souledge.

As a child, I danced these High Sierras,
dipped a dented cup into a stream, slaked
my thirst, drank again, fished a purple lake,

caught an eleven-inch Rainbow Trout, saw
my father stretch it another inch so he could
brag it was a full foot. All of this beside a fire
whose smoke remembers everything.

They're there, aren't they, memories fossilized
in the part of your heart that turned to stone,
the sun baking everything hard and dry except
for the nearby stream.

The water is there, isn't it? Dip your dented
cup, let the years silk your hand, slake your thirst,
soften stone.
Drink.

—E.C.

HAVE YOU CHANGED?

We begin to die the day we are silent about things that matter.

—Martin Luther King Jr.

PBS has been rerunning their great series *Eyes on the Prize*, chronicling key events in the Civil Rights movement of the 1950s and '60s. One of my regrets in life is that I didn't find the courage to join those marchers when I was in college and law school in the '60s. My reflection about that time caused me to wonder something each of us may ask: Have we changed? Would I find the courage to join a similar kind of march today? Or would I remain "silent about things that matter"?

In a broader sense, how *are* we different now than we were, say, five years ago? As caregivers, have we matured in our ability to give love, or have we become more bitter and burned out?

What's surprising is how infrequently most of us ask ourselves these questions. Is it because we are afraid of the answers? As one recent ad for an insurance company says, "Life comes at you fast..." Each day, each hour, each moment sails by. So much of our day may be filled with tasks that we may often find ourselves asking on a given birthday, "Where has the time gone?" And this question may serve to remind us of the importance of the need for quiet reflection on our lives.

Most people tell me they can't pause to do even the five-minute reflections I recommend because they just don't have the time. But those who are wise enough to take time to meditate each day experience a richer *quality* of life. Meditation improves our ability to be present. So does the practice of art appreciation. If we find ourselves wondering where all the time has gone, this means we've spent way too much time rushing through tasks and way too little time reflecting on the life we are living.

A century ago, Einstein proved that as an object approaches the speed of light, time actually slows down. In other words, time is not a function of the movement of the hands of the clock.

We know this in our everyday lives. Boring moments pass with agonizing slowness. Happy times evaporate faster than ice in summer.

How have we changed? My sister-in-law, Karen (pronounced Car-in, like the Norwegian) Updike is a poet. Her latest book, *This Holding On, This Letting Go*, was just published by Fireweed Press. I have seen Karen's

poetry change as she has aged. Her poems become better, stronger, richer with each effort. She has changed, and I hope my ability to appreciate her writing has improved as well, for art appreciation requires reflective pauses.

> *If growing old means showing more and more*
> *of our essential selves, let me hasten the process!*
> *Let me find the rip cord and the courage to use it!*

What a startling opening stanza. Who but a poet would think it was an advantage to *hasten* growing old? My daughter tells my wife and me on each birthday that we should be grateful for our age instead of complaining about it because we are, in fact, lucky to have lived as long as we have. She's right. And the greatest thing we may learn across life is the courage to be our truest selves. When, as King says, we are silent about things that matter, it may  mean that we are turning a blind eye to injustice. In so doing, some part of our soul breaks off and floats away. But we may yet find courage. As Karen writes in the next stanza of this poem, called "On Disappearing Cloaks":

> *Let me unravel all ruse, all hypocrisy*
> *by which we keep others from knowing us*
> *and us from knowing ourselves.*

Okay, I think I get the part about trying to honest and open to others. But I had forgotten the part about how lying to others can cause us to lie about ourselves so effectively that we no longer know who we are.

> *Let the nap be worn away, let the patterns emerge,*
> *etched and luminescent, like flowers*
> *in a prized Persian carpet.*

For poets, patterns are never just patterns, they must be illuminated for us as "flowers/ in a prized Persian carpet." What a gift she gives us by helping us sense the presence of our truest patterns by imagining the particular feel of flowers in a Persian rug. And finally,

> *Let the cloak become, not shabby, but transparent.*
> *Let our spirits glow, let everyone know*
> *that what they see is what in fact we are.*

Who are we now compared to a month ago, a year ago, a decade ago? How have we changed? Are there patterns we are caught in that we may shed? What kind of courage do we need to find the kind of transparency that will let everyone know who we really are?

We have all gained a certain comfort hiding within the elaborate cloaks and intricate masks we wear each day. It is hard to be present to many things that matter. It is difficult to speak truth to power.

Perhaps, today, we can begin to remove these masks, one at a time, and in the process, discover a truth we may have lost sight of on the long road to becoming adults—that underneath all the cloaks and the masks, there is something more beautiful and true than we ever realized.

And perhaps, on this journey, we may find the capacity not only for greater transparency, but for a deeper ability, as caregivers, to offer to others the love that shines through the transparency of our renewed selves.

SECRET THANKS

We never speak our deepest gratitude because it cannot be spoken.

Instead, as you sit around the table amid the chatter and the candles and the sweet potatoes that exhale their aroma the way fog rises from a slumbering pond, there will be a time of thanksgiving when you will write, on the hidden walls of your heart, in the space between the scars, secret letters.

And no one will know that you are giving thanks:

to the teacher that winked at you in the third grade signaling from her powerful throne that you were magic;

to the person who brushed the back of your hair with his anxious hand sending waves of life through your heart;

to the child whose birth gave you life and to your mother;

to the friend who sat silent with you as you wept your way back to courage;

to the cloud that swept back the hem of her skirt last Tuesday morning to reveal the sun;

to the oak leaf that lay patiently on the ground waiting for you to see her dorsal fin before she swam away on the wind;

to the patient who soft-eyed her thanks right before you never saw her again;

to the grandfather you never met as he smiles at you from the curtain near the six-paned window;

to your heart, even as she throws a slender shadow across your gratitude and you mourn the absence of those not there.

We never speak our deepest gratitude because it cannot be spoken. But we can send secret notes to our Thanksgiving ghosts.

—E.C.

OUR SEASON OF CHANGE

O leaf, you give your gifts freely to me. Why have I not seen your riches before?

—E.C.

September. Summer rustles her green skirt, rises to leave her place at the head of the table of seasons. In the Colorado Rockies, the Aspens surrender their emerald and give way to gold. From Idaho, across the Midwest and up into Maine, oak leaves set sail on their final journey. Across the southern United States, summer hesitates, stays her warm hand on the faces of days. Along the California coast, it's hard to tell when summer ends and fall begins.

However many years you have lived, you can multiply that by four. If you've lived forty years, you've seen one hundred sixty seasons come and go. Or have you? Did most of them slip from your view unnoticed? Did you find yourself living most of your springs beneath fluorescent lights, most of your winters indoors?

It's hard to stay present to the seasons if we've spent most of our lives chasing from one goal to the next. Yet when people enter their final days, what do they miss most? Most people don't wish they'd spent more time making money. Knowing they have fewer days, they find ways to put more time into each one by slowing the pace of their lives, by taking time to be present not only to the seasons but to their own lives.

There's no need for us to wait until our final days to live our lives. Today, do something you may not have done since you were a child. Sit with a tree and be present to her. Don't worry, she's not going anywhere. Close your eyes for awhile underneath her branches. She won't mind. From

behind closed eyes, brush the edge of her dress with your hands. Discover the *textures* of green and gold.

I did this meditation with a tree across the street from the front of our home. I don't know what kind it is, but here in Tennessee, it's one of the first to lose its green. I've taken three pictures of one of its leaves for you to see. In the first image, you can see her face. The scar at two o'clock

makes her more interesting, I think. Look at how early fall has already embroidered her edges.

In the second image of her underside, her vein structure is even more apparent, flexing out as if wanting to burst through the skin. She shows more green/ blue than yellow from this point of view even though it's the same leaf taken in the identical light. The other side of her scar is flashing out instead of in.

In the final sideways view, this single leaf shows us she has yet another personality. She can mimic a butterfly! I didn't notice this until I looked at the picture. In the background, impatiens and begonias still bloom bright. In the foreground, this leaf seems about to fly from my hand to visit each of the flowers, and on from there back to her tree in the Amazon forest.

Okay. If you just can't stand to leave the office or are unable to leave your home to sample the riches of nature, at least do this: Close your eyes and imagine yourself along the path through the loveliest garden you can picture. Remember, there's no rush. During a five-minute meditation, you may be able to visit the lives of many flowers or to focus the entire five minutes on just one.

Open your heart to the masterpieces of nature and you will experience a season of change in your life, a time when you feel yourself easing out of the grip of daily demands and into the lap of Love. This meditation brings you present to this season in the world. You can let it be a mirror for you as a caregiver who knows that presence to beauty enables you to be more present to your patients.

Take these images with you across your day or find your own. These jewels are free and available to all whose hearts are open to the great gifts of life. Let these images be keys you carry with you. Keys that will open the door to your own season of change.

RAIN WATCHING

Rain can nourish our souls.

—E.C.

T he eyes of my daughter's and son-in-law's home in Boston stare over the tops of trees. Rainfall smears the windows. Wire mesh ensnares rain's drops. I watched it rain at their house one day and took this picture.

Open-eyed meditation may mean looking at things we normally ignore. Rain watching has no function. It does not involve doing anything the world counts as productive. No one is paid simply to rain watch. But the experience can be deeply restful. Meditation is about being, not doing. Rain watching means letting the close sky and the darker day wrap us in their shadows.

Some people dread rain. My mother taught me to love it—especially if it's accompanied by its occasional twins, thunder and lightning. To this day, she greets rain's arrival by scrunching up her shoulders, rubbing her hands together, and cooing, "Rain. Oh Goody!" She does that every rainy autumn as clouds huddle over northern Ohio and leaves fall along with raindrops.

How does rain affect your mood? Rain watching brings beauty as rain silvers grass, tree branches, flower petals, the surfaces of cars, the windows of a home.

So often, rain watching evokes, for me, Dr. William Carlos Williams's immortal fifteen-word poem: *So much depends upon a red wheel barrow, glazed with rain, beside the white chickens.* At first glance, this may seem like an odd combination of words to some. What's so important about a wheelbarrow covered with rain, and a bunch of chickens? But what is Williams saying to us? Notice, he says, the way rain *glazes* the wheelbarrow. Be present to its red. Discover that there are white chickens nearby. Be present to all of this and pause in meditation over how to be present to the power of what is before you *in this moment.*

While the rest of us may describe something simply as "beautiful," poets find words we may have never thought of and, in so doing, enrich the experience of life. This is the gift of poetry for busy caregivers: to pause long enough to let the poetry reach our hearts, to let it help us be present to the images and people around us, to watch something without asking about its use, to live in appreciation of things that reach our senses and trigger within us small comets of joy.

Dr. Williams (1883–1963) was a physician as well as a poet. His genius as a caregiver was to let poetry inform his healing skills. His genius as a poet was his ability to convert his gifts of observation into words that live among the greatest literature of the 20th century. His poetry made him, and those who read his work with an open heart, better caregivers. Dr. Williams understood that great poetry explains how we see and how we feel. He knew that poetry can open a window to the soul of caregivers.

OCTOBER'S SCENT

The day flicks sparks of autumn into my eyes. October has a different scent.

The other side of spring is things dying so why does October's breath smell so fresh? In the hills, the earth puffs the smoke of summer's remains. Clouds search the curved horizon for a place to hide.

October wears a different scent. I will be present to her today.

I pull on her sweater, breathe her musk. In the Hospice blocks away, this is the last autumn for the woman in the pink robe who reaches for her jacket, slips it on, shuffles into the court-yard on limbs tired as old oaks. She leans into the sun, breathes the aroma of her last October.

In the hospital across the street, a new person breathes his first breath, inhales his first fall, the first days of his earth journey. His mother smiles out the window. Flicks of autumn spark her eyes. She knows October has a different scent . . .

Today we will talk of energy—the river of love that flows down the mountains past the shedding Aspens. She invites us to baptize ourselves in her water and to lift diamond droplets to drape the necks of those in need. Her water is alive with the only energy that can slake our thirst. She reminds us of the living water.

Today we will talk of intelligence—
the things my hands know,
the genius of your eyes,
the wide brilliance of your arms,
how smart you are to know, in your being,
what my being needs.

Today we will talk of presence—
the way you enter my room,
quiet as an angel, sit near me,
draw away some of my pain,
shift it onto your smooth shoulders,
share with me the communion of suffering.

Tonight, we will talk of light as the sun collapses into the
October hills. October has a different scent. We will breathe
her together. The coming night is our friend. We will welcome
her to our circle, listen as she reads to us October's story.

At midnight, we will dream our own dreams and each
other's. Dream-flying over October, we will land on the shoul-
der of the woman in the pink robe and whisper relief. We will
alight near the tiny baby and sing
a lullaby.

We will lie in moonlight by October's river
as she flows beneath the Aspens.
We will sip her night scent.
We will drink a glass of autumn,
And celebrate Love's gifts.

—E.C.

COMFORT FOR CAREGIVERS

The Comfort of Fog

I wish the morning fog, whose cotton hands
cling to trees and clothe every bush, would stay
all day and through this night.

I wish she would keep her cloak close
around me, ghost each window
as I walk about my home.

She softens all the edges, rounds
off the fence posts, silvers
the skin of leaves.

Beyond her arms, on the other side
of her pillowed body, the world
calls for my help.

This morning mist swallows
words in her
sighs.

Let me hide here
in her a little
longer,

grow stronger
in the comfort
of fog.

—E.C.

BEAUTY'S THORNS

Here again is the rose I introduced to you on page 144. I've been looking at the same black-and-white photograph of this flower every day for many years. I took the picture more than twenty-five years ago in Kenosha, Wisconsin. The rose was cut from my mother-in-law's garden and hangs on the wall next to the bathroom mirror. I watch this flower while shaving in the morning and while brushing my teeth in the evening. She never moves. She is always the same, and she is always different.

What can you see in a flower after the first few glances? To me, this flower is all texture and contour and shadows. She is also as intricate as a dancer and as multi-faceted as an aria. Look at how she poises in mid-darkness, her face angled toward the light, her many contours catching the light in ways more complex than a diamond.

One of the hardest things to understand about beauty is how much pain sits next to its joy. Look at this rose again. Inside its beauty do you not also feel some sense of pain? Not only the awareness of the thorns that warn you to touch carefully, but the knowing that beauty often draws tears with its joy.

Each patient or client in need—the patient with cancer, the child that has been abused, the homeless woman—is beautiful because he or she is human. When they are in pain, they remain beautiful and the compassionate among us feel the thorns of their pain and do not turn back. I admire and love the patients and caregivers of this world. I think they are gorgeous beings. Caregivers bring their love and attention to complete strangers—and they do it for inadequate pay. Some may think of doctors as rich. But in my thirty years of experience, I find that most physicians are underpaid for the hard and dedicated work they do to bring healing to those in need. The best caregivers embrace the beauty of the rose knowing they will sometimes suffer the wounds of her thorns.

The more beautiful the caregiver's work, the more likely it is to hold pain as well as joy. Human beings in need resemble roses. Their humanity makes us want to reach out to them. This is what Mother Teresa and other lesser-known lovers see when they look into the faces of the poor and the weak. And the more vulnerable they are, the more they take on other characteristics that lie beneath the face of the rose. It is the business of a rose to be beautiful. And it is her nature to wear thorns as well. That is why the best caregivers need such great courage. Love is beautiful and love hurts.

The Business of a Rose

Nothing hurts the soft surface
of my fingertips as does the betrayal
of her thorns.
All I wanted was to tip
her close enough
to taste.
But I was rude. I should have
folded my hands behind my back
in the manner of a museum patron,
a scientist studying a specimen,
or a suitor not yet permitted
to touch.
I should have polite-leaned instead
of sweeping her to me as if the two
of us were married.
It is the business of a rose to hurt.
Not only the thorns that soldier her spine,
but her leaves, her lips, the way the breeze stirs
her negligée, the curl of her rain-wet tongue,
the shadows that shade-light her skin,
the way she sways on her stem.
The business of a rose is to hurt:
the thorns, the leaves' edges,
and then her face, her heart-
tearing beauty,
her scent.

—E.C.

HOW MUCH DO WE LOVE?
HOW BEAUTIFUL IS A ROSE?

The effort to quantify love degrades it.

—E.C.

Think for a moment about someone you love. Describe this love. Then answer this question: How much do you love that person?

This question is often asked, yet it has a hollow ring to it. How can we possibly apply a measuring stick or a calculator to something as important to us as how much we love our spouse, or children or parents or best friends? In the case of saints like Mother Teresa, how can we quantify her love for the poorest of the poor?

The world of healthcare—particularly in hospitals—is dominated by science and, increasingly, business. Many people think that a key element of science is measurement. We all know that a central measure of business success is "the bottom line."

In such a world, it is not surprising that love slides rapidly down the priority list so that it is barely visible as an objective of organizations that hold themselves out as caring.

One reason for this is the seductive appeal of measurement. We seek the reinforcement of measurable goals so we migrate to areas where calculation is king. "How many milligrams of drug were administered to that patient and what was the result?" We ask this and revel in the fact that we can make an exact-seeming calculation of the impact of our actions. "How many patients were discharged from the hospital this month and what percentage were Medicare?" the Chief Financial Officer or the CEO may ask.

These are normal clinical and business inquiries. There is nothing wrong with these questions unless they become so dominant they entirely erode the role of the caring questions.

Leaders and caregivers may be asking, along with the above questions, *"How are we doing giving loving care?"* Some, confused by the scientific and business models, will seek to quantify the answer. Yes, it's possible to get some clues from tools like patient satisfaction surveys, but these reports can never answer the questions of ultimate importance.

"How are we giving loving care?" This is not a dosage question. No nurse can report that she administered 25ccs of kindness to an eighty-five-year-old. However, she can describe kind things she has done. She can say things like, "While taking Mr. Jones's blood pressure, I listened carefully as he told me about his wife's terminal cancer. And I stayed with him in his sorrow as he shed tears."

She can describe her gift of loving presence to the spiritual needs of another rather than quantifying it. I hate to quote a source as commercial as a television ad, but the Master Card people have it right when they calculate what a list of things costs and end their ad with their particular way of describing a given human experience: "Priceless."

This ad connects with the public because every person knows intuitively that the most important things in life have no price tag. If a credit card company can comprehend this, why is it so hard for leaders caught in the medical-industrial complex to appreciate the same wisdom?

Ask yourself what is most important—the things we can measure or the things that live beyond the measuring stick? We live near both the hard stick and the soft-petaled rose. Where is the balance? We don't need to know the exact answer. But we can find balance by asking the question every day.

AUTUMNAL EQUINOX

Those who are present to nature know that seasonal change is gradual, happening over many days. Yet there is a pivot point on the calendar. September 22 is the date when day and night are equal. Fall, as the gateway to winter, is a celebratory time for some and more difficult for others who fear the cold and darkness. If you can make out the moon tonight, you may celebrate it as the Wine Moon since this is the time of year when grapes are harvested. Wine Moon. The phrase has a pretty sound to me. And the word images we use have so much to do with how we feel about seasonal change.

For many years, starting at age twelve (my age when my family moved from southern California to northern Ohio), I disliked fall. I even came to dislike the word "crisp" because it was always the word my dad used to describe the first cool day. To me, the word was simply a reminder of warm California days that were no more. After some hard winters on the edge of Lake Erie, fall began to feel to me like a death sentence. In fact, something had died. I didn't know what that was at the time. But it was my childhood.

I liked being a teenager. But it was hard to surrender childhood and even harder to recognize I could never really return to California's near continuous diet of fair weather.

The main reason I've been drawn, recently, to the power of the Serenity Prayer is that I realize how many seasons I've wasted repeating useless patterns of regret and resentment over things I can't change. I lost the enjoyment of the stunning beauty of so many northern autumns because I allowed myself to be weighed down with mourning that I was in Ohio and not California. How foolish of me. No one ever helped me come to terms with my grieving and I never lived the solution myself until recently.

Once I truly began to absorb the wisdom of the Serenity Prayer, I began to wonder why so many of us allow our moods to be controlled by the weather outside instead of the light within. "Oh no, it's cloudy again," one nurse will report glumly to another. Hours later, she still looks glum, the clouds outside hanging over her head like a leaden cloak. Next day, it's sunny and she's smiling, her face a remarkable barometer.

"God grant me the serenity to accept the things I cannot change." If there was ever something that can't be changed, it's the weather of the moment. Does this mean we should all go around celebrating cloudy days? Perhaps it means that we accept dark weather with grace and focus our

energy on the joy of living and on changing the things we can change.

The Autumnal Equinox is a chance to meditate on balance. Many Japanese celebrate this day as a time to visit the graves of the dead—to honor the gifts and the light of those who have left this earth. In this celebration, they embrace loss with serenity.

Can the wisdom of the Serenity Prayer bring us a new season of joy? Can we find a better balance between work and rest?

Many caregivers, beset with worries about those in need, actually *fear* resting. Yet rest, reflection, and meditation are critical to balance and to good caregiving. As Wayne Mueller writes, service to others is challenging work, but it need not be "a painful and dreary thing." If it's beginning to seem dreary, it means things are out of balance.

When you breathe in the early taste of fall, you may smell the aroma of change. You may even decide, as have I, that each season's arrival is a time for celebrating life as it comes and goes. After all, the seasons will change whether we like it or not. So we have the choice to embrace the change with joy or to fuss about something outside our control.

I still miss California, but that small ache doesn't stop me from loving autumn in Tennessee, the state where my wife and I have lived since 1998.

Along the Sonoma and Napa Valleys, the grapes are ready for harvest. Here, shades of gold and red emerge in leaves once dressed only in green.

Tonight I'm going to stare up into the Nashville sky and celebrate the Wine Moon even if clouds block my view. All of life waits to be lived, not in fear but in love.

AUTUMN PURPLE

By following autumn's purple thread, we may come to appreciate even more of the beauty of nature and of life.

—E.C.

Beyond the fluorescent lights under which so many caregivers work, autumn births colors rare in the sterile environment of hospitals. In all the falls I've lived, I never noticed until this one how much purple emerges in October. I always think of this month as gold and red and yellow. But it's the purple I see this year.

Meditation allows us to see what we may not have noticed when we're in a hurry. CBS *Sunday Morning* recently presented the story of a *National Geographic* photographer. He spoke of traveling the world capturing stunning images for the magazine and the prizes he had won. Then his face softened. "My career was going great. But I was gone from home a lot. Then my wife found a lump. It was cancer. Everything changed."

This story has a good ending.

In the backwash of the horrors of chemotherapy, husband and wife rediscovered life *and* each other. And a father rediscovered his children. "Sometimes," he said, "my wife and I just sit outside at dusk and watch the night come on. We don't always say much. We just enjoy nature and each other." His wife will live. And they're both going to *live differently* from now on.

Why does it so often take a shock for us to discover the true beauty in life? Why haven't I ever noticed all the shades of purple that live in every autumn of every year? All of the images in this reflection I found and photographed within a hundred feet of my house.

Purple is a regal color. In ancient times, it was hard to come by purple cloth. Its rarity increased its significance. Only royalty was permitted to wear cloth of this special color.

One shade of purple called mauve happens to have a fascinating little history. The color did not exist in clothing until an odd incident in 1856 that ended up affecting medical as well as fashion history. A young scientist, William Perkin, was trying to develop a cure for malaria. In the course of trying to invent a synthetic form of quinine, he stumbled upon an oily black substance that, when purified and dried, became a lovely shade of

light purple. One can estimate that barely one in a million scientists would have had the insight to recognize that this accident had the potential to create a whole new kind of cloth that would transform fashion—not just clothing, but cosmetics. Perkin was wise enough to keep his thinking open. The spark of his genius even led to discoveries in photography and in medicine. All because he stayed present to an "accident" in his experimentation and had the brilliance to recognize what was before him.

Mauve has always been present in nature. So has the deeper purple of autumn. Human beings seek to dress themselves in various shades found in nature—as if we were all chameleons seeking to blend with our environment.

Yet it is the experience of autumn's purple we may reflect on today—not because we've never seen it before, but because it calls us to nature. In the midst of all the complex treatments we offer to patients trapped in illness, beyond all the blood and pain caregivers must face, this is a moment to sit back, breathe, and enjoy a special part of nature's show—her velvet displays of purple—in trees, in flowers, in precious stones, in the leaves we drive by on the way to work, in the sun's setting and in its rising.

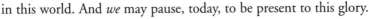

Purple. It's just a color. But it provides a chance for gratitude—for our eyesight, for nature, for fall, for the rich, silk quality of this regal shade. God's beauty is present in this world. And *we* may pause, today, to be present to this glory.

PARTINGS

I should be content
to look at a mountain
for what it is
and not as a comment
on my life.

—David Ignatow

I've written to you about leaves and roses and water fanning out from a garden hose across my backyard. In nature, poet David Ignatow thinks the idea is to be content with what we see, whether beautiful or scarred. It is our tendency to seek to fuss with and readjust nature. Cut flowers need to be arranged, we think. Dead leaves must be swept away. It's hard for us to leave the world alone—especially as she presents herself in our backyard. Parks we visit need to spread signs around warning us not to touch. Can we be content to observe the mountain or the rose for their strength and elegance and not as a comment on our lives?

Ignatow tells us he thinks he should be content just to look. This means it is his temptation to connect the meaning of the mountain to meaning in his own life, to take the presence of the mountain as some kind of personal commentary on his life. But we wonder if, standing there in its massive presence, he succeeds.

Sensitive caregivers are inclined to take the twists and turns in their patients' health as commentaries on their caregiving. I have often heard nurses say, upon the death of someone in their care, "My patient died on me." As if the patient had chosen to pass away as a direct insult to the caregiver.

When we are present to a patient's suffering, it is natural that some kind of blurring occurs in the line between patient and caregiver. This is why leaders often counsel the need for "boundaries."

I don't know if boundary discussions are helpful or not. What seems clear is that committed caregivers share in both pain and joy. This is apparent in hospital nurseries where caregivers welcome new life and in hospices where caregivers walk with their patients to the end of their path, holding their hands until they must let go.

Fall is a time of letting go. As a human being, I can't help but take that personally as I watch autumn commit its annual robbery, its killings in my backyard and along the road to work, its reminder of life beyond fluorescent lights.

October Leaf

Even though a trace of green
veins her new gold,
I know she is about to dive,
standing there on the edge

scared as a nine-year-old facing a first
big leap off the dock and into the lake;

excited as Archimedes about to hurl
himself from his bath mid-Eureka;

horrified as 17-year-old seamstress Rebecca
Feibish, window-ledged on the last day
of her life in 1911, by flames
ripping the floors of the Triangle Shirtwaist
Factory where she took her last stand.

I watch the leaf plan her flight path,
test the wind, survey the angle of the sun,
sniff for the presence of birds
whose wings might interfere,
recite her penance.

She fetches a final glance at her sisters
and brothers, bunched, staring back,
planning their own leaps.

It must be hard for her
to plan the trajectory
of a journey that will be
her first, her only,
her last.

—E.C.

THE MOST PERSONAL INVITATION

Come, now, to your place of rest.
Not your bed, for this is not about sleep.

Find a chair, a place on the floor, or a large log in the forest
lying on its side where it fell after all
those years of standing tall on the only spot it ever occupied in
the core of the deep woods.
Now its smooth bark offers itself to you.
See light as you have never seen it before—how it creates new
things through its shadows.
Why is the shadow not like its parent? Look at the shadow of
the twig, look how the sun changes
a hanger in this photograph I took in 1978.
Consider your own shadow and how it changes in the shifting
angles of sun and moon and Love.

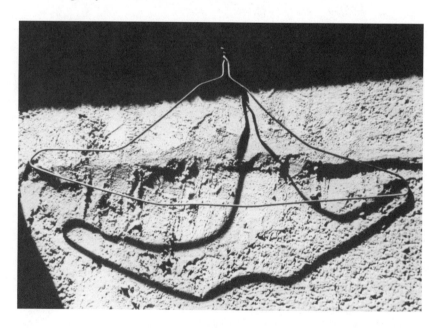

*Go, now, to that place within, the place where you sit at the
crossing, and watch the train of your
thoughts steaming by.
Before you close your eyes, you see.*

*There's the male cardinal in the evergreen.
You wait and watch, knowing she's nearby, and soon she appears,
shadowing her mate faithful as a Geisha.
But she is not her mate.*

*It is the nature of cardinals to mate for life.
But the shadow is not a copy of the thing it seems to mimic.
You are mated to yourself for
your journey across this world but are you divorced
from yourself?
Are your travels marked by speed? As you watch your
life are you
startled by your own velocity—by the difference between
your shadows and yourself?
If you love your life, why are you so anxious to rush
through it?
The finish line will come and the prize goes not to the
fastest, the craftiest, the richest, or the one who was the busiest.*

*Your shadow is not you.
Your shadows have their own fascinating forms
and each shape is cut from the outline of the light around you.*

*Here is your chance.
You are a caregiver who can decline, as you may
have in the past, the old invitation sitting there on
the table with the bills and the third-class mail addressed to
Occupant.*

*But this is your personal invitation addressed not to your
shadow but only to you.
Today you can choose to accept the invitation to live your one
and only life
on your terms—the terms outlined and filled in by Love's light.*

Come, now, to Love's invitation.
Sit, rest, breathe.
Nothing matters more than the
pair of cardinals
hopping limb to limb.
Nothing matters more than the cedars swaying to the tune
of the wind.
Nothing matters more than the rhythm of your breath
and the people
out there you will be able to love because you accepted this
chance to rest.

Busy fingers fall still; eyelids close to the song of daylight, the
music of dusk.
The distant click of your Blessing Train glides down the track
of your life,
comes to a stop, unloads its passengers onto the platform where
you greet each, not
all at once but one by one, as if now is the only time and
today is your holiday.

Today become a guest at your own table of Thanksgiving.
Sit with all of your
different-shaped shadows.
Celebrate each with open arms.
Pick one to revisit awhile.

There they are—all your gifts, all your best angels, all your
beautiful shadows carved
from light and gathered in the circle of your love.
Come, rest, rejoice in Love's glorious invitation.

Say kind things to your shadows and to every person you
encounter today.

What you do to others, you do to yourself.
So be a lover and watch Love flood your heart.

—Erie Chapman

ABOUT THE AUTHOR

Erie Chapman, M.T.S., J.D., is president and chief executive officer of the Baptist Healing Trust, Nashville, Tennessee. Mr. Chapman is acknowledged by many as the leader of the Loving Care Movement in America. His first book, *Radical Loving Care,* is now in its seventh printing and is changing the way healthcare is delivered in America, along with the followup *Sacred Work: Planting Cultures of Radical Loving Care in America.* Across Mr. Chapman's extraordinary career he has served as a successful trial attorney, federal prosecuting attorney, night court judge, producer/host of an internationally syndicated television show, publisher of a healthcare magazine, newspaper columnist, radio talk show host, documentary film producer, and author. Recent projects include the narration of the *Radical Loving Care* audiobook and editing the online *Journal of Sacred Work* (www.journalofsacredwork.typepad.com). He is also a prize-winning photographer and a music composer. He is a graduate of Vanderbilt University Divinity School and a veteran hospital CEO.

The primary focus of Mr. Chapman's career, however, has been in the leadership of hospitals and healthcare organizations. Over twenty-five years of his career, he served as President and CEO of Riverside Hospital in Toledo, Ohio (at age 33), Riverside Methodist Hospital in Columbus, Ohio (1983-1995), the nine-hospital U.S. Health Corporation (now OhioHealth) in Columbus (founding president and CEO), chief operating officer of the publicly traded InPhyNet Medical Management Co., Ft. Lauderdale, and Baptist Hospital System, Nashville, where he served as President and CEO from 1998–2002. Erie and his wife, Kirsten, a prize-winning journalist and author of *The Way Home* and *Home Again,* live in Nashville. They have two children and one grandchild.

Baptist Healing Trust
1919 Charlotte Ave.
Nashville, TN 37203
www.healinghospital.org